Basil Edward Hammond

The Political Institutions of the Ancient Greeks

Basil Edward Hammond

The Political Institutions of the Ancient Greeks

ISBN/EAN: 9783337070625

Printed in Europe, USA, Canada, Australia, Japan

Cover: Foto ©Suzi / pixelio.de

More available books at **www.hansebooks.com**

THE POLITICAL INSTITUTIONS
OF THE ANCIENT GREEKS.

BY

BASIL EDWARD HAMMOND

FELLOW AND LECTURER, TRINITY COLLEGE, CAMBRIDGE:
UNIVERSITY LECTURER IN HISTORY.

LONDON:
C. J. CLAY AND SONS,
CAMBRIDGE UNIVERSITY PRESS WAREHOUSE,
AVE MARIA LANE.

1895

[All Rights reserved.]

PREFACE.

THESE chapters are not intended to form a whole by themselves. They are merely an enlarged version of a course of lectures in which European Political Institutions in general were treated historically and comparatively: and as I wish hereafter to make similar enlarged versions of the other parts of the course and to append them to what I have here written, I hope that these chapters on the Greek Institutions may prove to be only a first instalment of a book on Comparative Politics. The following pages contain what their title indicates, a description and examination of Greek governments: but in view of the additions which may probably be made to them, they also contain a small amount of matter which is necessary as a preliminary to an examination of European governments in general.

The attention which I have paid to method and definitions of terms might lead my readers to suppose that I conceive Comparative Politics to be a science. It is only fair to them to express the opinions that I have formed on the matter. I do think that the part of the comparative study of Politics, which deals with barbaric and more particularly with non-European peoples and their governments, has been placed on a scientific footing by Mr Herbert Spencer in his

Political Institutions, though he has attained this great result by a method which is not purely comparative, and which, as it takes no heed of historical sequence of events, has not stood him in good stead where he treats of historical European communities and their constitutions. The part—the most interesting and important part—of the study, that which is concerned with civilised peoples and governments, seems to me not yet to be science. It does indeed enable us to lay down empirical rules, or rules founded solely on observation, about peoples and governments, just as the study of a language enables a grammarian to lay down empirical rules about words and sentences. And further, among the rules which have been laid down, there are some, (their number is, I believe, very small,) which seem to be distinguished from the rest in two respects, firstly because they are not subject to any known exception, and secondly because some of the causes which lie at the root of them have been discovered: and these rules have something of the character of scientific laws, or rules which are true, not only in all known instances, but universally. But, on the other hand, most of the rules which have as yet been laid down are of a different sort, and, either because they are vague and indefinite, or because they are subject to many exceptions, or for other like reasons, nothing of the nature of a scientific law has been founded on them.

It is however common to all studies to be imperfect and only half conclusive while they are in their infancy: many studies, especially among those which are based on comparisons, have before now progressed within the lapse of a few generations from a very lowly condition to the status of complete inductive sciences: and it is hard to see why the same good fortune should not at some future time fall to the lot of Comparative Politics.

The classification of European political bodies, which is

given in my second chapter, was suggested to me in its main outlines by a lecture which I heard delivered in Cambridge many years ago by my friend Sir John Seeley: the usefulness of some such classification was made clear to me some years later but yet long ago by a course of lectures which was given by another friend Professor Henry Sidgwick: and I have constructed the classification as it stands in the second chapter with the intention of making it serve as a framework both for what I have here written about the Greeks and their governments and for what I hope to write hereafter about other European peoples and governments. To both the gentlemen whom I have named I desire to express my hearty thanks for the help and guidance that their lectures have given me in my attempts to study Politics methodically.

B. E. HAMMOND.

TRINITY COLLEGE, CAMBRIDGE.
December 12, 1894.

CONTENTS.

CHAPTER		PAGE
I.	The Aryan Races	1
II.	A Classification of European Political Bodies . .	8
III.	Greek Political Institutions. Heroic Monarchies	23
IV.	Sparta	37
V.	The Greek Cities	57
VI.	Aristotle's Classification of Polities . .	99
VII.	The Achæan League	114

ERRATUM.

Page 14, line 21, *for* empires *read* empire.

CHAPTER I.

THE ARYAN RACES.

It is proved by similarities in the languages of the European peoples and the Hindus and the Persians that they had in some sense a common origin. It is not indeed probable that they are sprung from the same parents: but their ancestors once formed a group of closely associated peoples who lived beside one another as neighbours and used either the same language or dialects of the same language. The peoples which had in this sense a common origin comprise all those that belong to the stocks of the Hindus, the Persians, the Celts, the Greeks, the Italians, the Teutons and the Slavs, and are known collectively as the Aryans or as the Indo-European peoples.

The evidence of language not only proves that the Aryans lived together as neighbours, but also tells us something about their pursuits and habits. From the languages of the Greeks, the Romans, the Germans and the ancient Hindus we learn that the forefathers of these peoples before they left their common dwelling-place were acquainted with the most important domestic animals and had a name for each of them: for the words *cow*, German *Kuh*, Sanskrit *gâus*, Greek βοῦς, Latin *bos*, are mere variations from an Aryan word whose meaning they retain unaltered: the same is true of the word *ewe*, Sanskrit *avis*, Greek ὄϊς, Latin *ovis*; of *goose*, German *Gans*, Sanskrit *hansas*, Greek χήν, Latin *anser*; of *sow*, German *Sau*, Sanskrit *sû*, Greek σύς or ὗς, Latin *sus*; of *hound*, German *Hund*,

H.

Sanskrit *çvan*, Greek κύων, Latin *canis*; and of Sanskrit *açvas*, Greek ἵππος, Latin *equus*, Saxon *eoh* or *ehu*.

In like manner the words *door*, German *Thüre*, Sanskrit *dvaras*, Greek θύρα, Latin *fores*, prove that the Aryans used a word bearing the same meaning and therefore their dwellings were something more than mere tents or moveable huts. *Yoke*, German *Joch*, Sanskrit *jugam*, Greek ζυγόν, Latin *jugum*, prove that they employed cattle for draught; ἄξων, Latin *axis*, Sanskrit *akshas* (axle and cart), Old High German *ahsa* (axle) indicate the use of carts; the Sanskrit *nâus*, Greek ναῦς, Latin *navis*, German *Nachen*, show that they could make boats: the Sanskrit *aritram* (an oar or paddle[1]), Greek ἐρετμός, Latin *remus* (*resmus*), prove that they propelled them by rowing or paddling. The absence however of common words for a mast, a sail, the sea, indicate that the waters that they knew were rivers or small lakes and that they did not possess the art of getting propulsion from the wind[2].

The Aryans were not entirely ignorant of plants that produce corn: for there was an Aryan word from which are descended the Sanskrit *yavas* (barley), the Greek ζειά (spelt, a kind of grain) and *jáva* in Zend (or Old Persian), Slavic and Lithuanian. Mommsen, noticing only the Sanskrit and the Greek, and observing the difference of meaning, thinks that the Aryans while they were all together merely gathered and ate the grains of barley and spelt that grew wild. A recent English writer points out the wide diffusion of the words descended from the Aryan word, and thinks it could not have left traces of its existence in so many languages unless corn had been cultivated by the Aryans and had thus become well known to them[3]. This inference seems to be fair: but

---

[1] See Curtius, *Grundzüge der Griechischen Etymologie*, under the word ἀρόω.

[2] The evidence derived from comparison of the Greek, Latin and Sanskrit is taken from Mommsen, *History of Rome*, English translation, vol. I. p. 15: the additional evidence from German languages from Max Müller, *Chips from a German Workshop*, vol. II. pp. 22, 44. Curtius, *Grundzüge der Griechischen Etymologie*, has been used for verification.

[3] Mommsen, *Hist. Rome*, vol. I. p. 16. Rendall, *The Cradle of the Aryans*, p. 11.

the absence of traces of other original Aryan words for agricultural products or instruments shows clearly that agriculture played only a subordinate part in their economy. It is probable that they sowed some kind of grain in little plots of ground that scarcely needed tillage.

The results of the evidence which has been adduced may be summed up by saying that the forefathers of the Greeks, Romans, Germans and Hindus, while they still occupied their common Aryan home, lived not in tents but in houses with doors, and were therefore not mere wanderers but had more or less permanent abodes: they were not savages dependent on wild animals and wild fruits for subsistence, but had sheep and cattle to supply them with flesh and milk: they had carts on wheels and knew how to yoke their oxen and horses: they made boats and propelled them on their rivers or lakes with oars or paddles: and they were acquainted with some kinds of grain, but were either ignorant of agriculture or cared little for it.

From the condition in which the Aryans lived we may safely infer that they were not totally devoid of political institutions. All men live under government except a few to whom government is either impossible or useless. The multitude of uncivilised races who inhabit or have inhabited the earth may be divided into two great classes; the first and lower class consisting of those who depend for subsistence solely on wild plants and wild animals, the second and upper class comprising all those who, in addition to the wild fruits that they may gather and the wild animals that they may kill, also have tame cattle to supply them with flesh and milk or cultivated plants that produce grain. The lower class are known either as savages or as hunting peoples: the upper, for want of a better name, may be designated as barbarians. In the lower class, the savages and hunting peoples, a very small number of peoples are found who have been prevented by specially adverse circumstances from having any governments: but in the rest of the lower class and in all the upper class of uncivilised peoples the existence of some kind of government is universal.

In illustration and proof of these statements some facts may be cited. The Bushmen of South Africa were at the beginning of the present century a race of savages who wandered over an arid sloping plain that lies to the South of the Orange River. They just contrived to maintain a miserable existence on the roots that they could grub up and on the flesh of animals that they shot with poisoned arrows or entrapped in pitfalls: but, as every family was compelled to keep itself isolated from all neighbours in order to have enough to eat, government was impossible. Other races resembling the Bushmen in the isolation of their families and in having no government are the Rock Veddahs in Ceylon and the Digger Indians in California. A slightly different case occurs in the regions near the North Pole. The Esquimaux, who live by catching seals and other marine animals, are not precluded from grouping their huts in small clusters: but nature offers so little reward to any combined effort of a large number of men that they have never cared to form political communities: and they afford perhaps the only example of human beings living as neighbours but without government. Leaving these very exceptional cases, we next observe a group of hunting peoples with whom nature dealt less unkindly. Some forty years ago, almost the only inhabitants of the western part of British North America, now known as Manitoba, were a number of Red Indian tribes who supported themselves entirely by the chase, killing buffalo for food and other animals for their furs, which they passed on to traders in return for such commodities as the traders brought them. During the greater part of the year each Red Indian family wandered almost as much apart from communication with mankind as did the Bushmen, for so the wild animals could most advantageously be pursued: and of course while they remained in dispersion had no government. But at certain seasons in every year a whole tribe came together for a great buffalo hunt: at other times they assembled to organize a war against some neighbouring tribe: and whenever they met for either purpose they subjected themselves to an efficient government, which included even a system of police. Apart from the groups of peoples whom I have mentioned, no great number of savage peoples seems to have been observed in recent times: the New Zealanders when first the Europeans went among them were savages and cannibals, and yet they lived under well established kingly governments.

With regard to the upper class of uncivilised peoples, the barbarians, who either keep cattle or grow corn or do both, it will suffice to say that observation of all of them (and they are extremely numerous) proves that all of them have governments. Nor is the fact hard to understand: for in their case it is never necessary for single families to live in isolation: they do as a matter of fact live collected together in groups of families, and each group gains numberless advantages by living together and acting together: and, where men live together and act together, government naturally comes into existence. Those of the barbarian peoples who, like the Aryans, have more or less fixed abodes, always group themselves in small independent tribes and adopt such simple forms of government as are suited to their circumstances. There are many different kinds of tribal governments. In nearly all of them a small number of men distinguished for prowess daring or intelligence have some authority over the rest: sometimes above these chiefs there is a higher chief or king: and sometimes the whole body of warriors may be called together to hear what the chiefs have to say to them. Among the ancient Aryans all the governments were no doubt tribal governments: but it is impossible to say that any one of the various kinds of tribal governments prevailed to the exclusion of the rest[1].

[1] The classification of uncivilised peoples as hunting peoples and peoples with cattle forms part of the classification used by John Stuart Mill at the beginning of his *Political Economy*: and it is adopted and fully worked out by Mr Lewis Morgan in his *Ancient Society*.

All the statements of a general kind which I have made about uncivilised peoples have been verified by reference to *Descriptive Sociology, Division I.*, an encyclopædia of facts relating to such peoples, which was designed by Mr Herbert Spencer and compiled by Professor Duncan. The advantages which uncivilised men gain from living and acting together and from having a government are explained by Mr Herbert Spencer in his *Political Institutions*, §§ 440—442.

My authorities for the individual peoples which have been noticed are these:

When the Aryans had made such progress as I have described they divided into two groups: one group contained the forefathers of the Europeans, the other the forefathers of the Hindus and Persians. Whether the separation arose through a migration of only the Europeans or of only the Asiatics or from migrations of both Europeans and Asiatics cannot be determined. It is certain however that after the division of the stocks took place the Europeans still remained together long enough to acquire in common the art of ploughing. The English word to *ear*, Anglo-Saxon *erian*, Gothic *erjan*, Old High German *eren*, Latin *arare*, Greek ἀρόειν, Irish *araim* (I plough) are mere variations of a single word and show that when ploughing was introduced the European stocks were still in close neighbourhood with one another and all adopted dialectic varieties of the same sound to indicate the new method of breaking up the soil[1].

The region in which the forefathers of the Europeans lived together cannot be precisely ascertained: the hypothesis that it was in central Europe seems to fit in best with the geographical distribution of their descendants and the relationships between their languages.

The invention of the art of ploughing opened new possibilities for the European peoples: for an agricultural people has far better chances than a people of herdsmen of accumulating wealth and making progress in the useful arts. But not all of them cared to make use of the new art and to become tillers of the soil. Those who took their homes amid the forests of central Europe still continued the life of hunters and herdsmen

for the Bushmen, Burchell, *Travels* (1822), and Thompson, *Travels* (1827): for the Esquimaux, C. F. Hall, *Life with the Esquimaux* (1864): for the Red Indians, H. Y. Hind, *The Canadian Red River Exploring Expedition* (1860). All these books are cited in *Descriptive Sociology*.

[1] It may be objected that the Goths from about 250 A.D. were living close to the Greeks, and the Old Germans from about 50 B.C. had the Romans as their neighbours, and possibly learned the art of ploughing from these neighbours and borrowed a name for it. It seems enough, however, to answer that if the Goths had taken a word from ἀρόειν they would have chosen something more like the pattern word than *erjan*: in like manner if the Germans had borrowed from *arare* they would hardly have formed *eren*.

which had once been common to all the Aryans. Others devoted themselves to agricultural pursuits with delight and success: and among them were those who settled in the peninsulas of Greece and Italy, where, favoured by many circumstances, they made comparatively rapid progress in arts, knowledge and political development.

CHAPTER II.

A CLASSIFICATION OF EUROPEAN POLITICAL BODIES.

THE subject matter of the study of politics consists firstly of the groups or collections of men who have lived under governments, and secondly of the governments under which they have lived. In the present chapter I wish to speak of the groups, to describe in outline the various forms which they have taken, and to define the names by which their forms are severally known. I must premise that I shall call some of the groups political communities, meaning by a political community a number of persons living under one government and also having much else in common besides government: the rest I shall call political aggregates, meaning by a political aggregate a number of persons or bodies of persons living under one government and having nothing else or very little else in common. Having said this, I can proceed to notice the forms of individual communities or aggregates, with a view to classifying them according to their forms. In my survey the earliest forms will be taken first, and the others afterwards, as far as possible in chronological order[1].

---

[1] I have thought it needless in most cases to give authorities for statements of historical facts made in this chapter, because the statements are generally such that it is very easy to settle whether they are true or false. In cases where verification might be in the least degree difficult I have given references.

The two European races into whose past we can grope our way farthest back are the Germans and the Greeks. Each of these races, when first we have any knowledge of them, had formed a large number of tribes or small primitive political communities. The German tribes in the times of Cæsar and of Tacitus and the Greek tribes in the time of Homer were alike in being of small size and in being primitive in their habits and government: but in a German tribe the whole population lived scattered over the open country and there was no walled city, while in a Greek tribe, though most of the people lived in the open country, there was a walled city as a centre for the community and a dwelling place for a few of the most important tribesmen. It is desirable to give the word *tribe* such a definition as will emphasize the distinction between a tribe and a city, and I shall therefore define it as meaning a small primitive political community, living in the open country without any walled city. From this definition it follows that I must regard the German tribes alone as being perfect specimens of the genus tribe or as being tribes pure and simple: the early Greek communities, though for brevity I shall speak of them as tribes, ought in strict accuracy to be regarded as tribes which were on the way to become cities and which had already acquired some small portion of the qualities by which cities are characterized.

In Greece tribes were succeeded by cities, that is to say small communities in which a walled city is everything, and the country districts are of little importance: and similar communities arose also in Italy. The cities of ancient Greece and Italy are often further designated as city-states, and the name is rightly applied to them: for they were not only cities in the sense which I have given to the word, but were also states because each of them was an independent community with a government of its own.

But the cities of ancient Greece and Italy were not all alike: the Greek cities were inexpansive: in Italy one city expanded itself by conquering a host of other cities and absorbing their populations into its own body politic. The contrast between the inexpansive cities of Greece and the expansive city of Rome is a matter of which I hope some time to speak at length: for the present it will suffice to notice that the Athenians, the largest political community known to Greek history in the age of the city states (that is to say before 338 B.C.), inhabited a territory of less area than an average English county: while in Italy before the beginning of the second Punic war (218 B.C.) towns or fortresses peopled by fully qualified citizens of the Roman Republic were to be found scattered over all the central region from Sena Gallica in Umbria to Sinuessa in Campania, and other towns or fortresses whose inhabitants possessed the private but not the public rights of Roman citizens existed in all parts of the peninsula[1]. It must however be observed that Rome did not by its expansion lose the distinguishing characteristics of a city state: it still continued after its expansion over all Italy to be a community in which a single city was of supreme importance and the population remote from the city was, politically at least, of little moment: but as it was incomparably larger than any ordinary city state, we must call it not simply a city state but an enlarged or expanded city state.

The small size of the Greek cities and their incapacity for acting in concert led to their subjugation by Macedonia in 338 B.C. About sixty or eighty years later many of them had recovered their independence, and some of them, in order to guard against a second conquest by Macedonia, joined together in a league or federation. The union of many communities in a federation was not a new thing in Greek history: during several centuries that preceded the year 338 B.C. some obscure tribes of mountaineers (the Achæans) had lived in such a union; their league had been broken up by the Macedonian conquerors, but they had been able, about 281 B.C., to reconstitute it: and the Greek cities, when they began, about 251 B.C., to see their need of mutual defence, had the Achæan League ready at hand, and were able to gain what they needed by

---

[1] Marquardt, *Römische Staatsverwaltung*, Vol. I. pages 22–57, in the edition of 1873, comprising the section headed *Italien vor der lex Julia*. Mommsen, *History of Rome*, Vol. II., especially the *Military Map of Italy* at the beginning of the volume.

enrolling themselves among its members. The Achæan League, enlarged by the admission of many important cities, was a federal state: that is to say, it was a community in which each city or canton had a government of its own for most purposes, but the federation or union of cities and cantons had also a common government for those matters which most nearly concerned the safety of them all. The League was perfectly successful till 221 B.C. in attaining the ends for which it had been established, and is remarkable as furnishing the first example in history of a well organized federal state[1].

The Romans employed the strength, which they had acquired through their conquest of Italy and their success in the second Punic war, in getting possession of many distant territories inhabited by alien races. Before 146 B.C. they were masters of Macedonia, part of Asia Minor, Spain and northern Africa, and the Roman dominions presented an example of a mere political aggregate, or heterogeneous empire or number of peoples having no natural attraction for one another and held together only by force. For the rule of a heterogeneous empire the institutions of a city and even of an expanded city proved utterly unsuitable: and it was necessary that both the conquering city and the dominions which it had conquered should submit to be ruled under a centralised and despotic system of government adapted to the needs of a heterogeneous empire. The right system was only gradually made, but it had been completed by the death of the Emperor Constantine the Great in 337 A.D.

But it is time to return to the Germans: for the Germans were the successors of the Romans as masters of Western Europe. The Germans in their primitive tribal condition possessed a great aptitude for forming large political communities by the union of many small communities:—an aptitude which is probably common to all peoples in a tribal condition:—and they inhabited a flat country which put no obstacles in the way of the amalgamation of their tribes. At any rate the German tribes between 150 A.D. and 400 A.D. were

[1] For details see Chapter VII.

engaged in a process of amalgamation. About 150 A.D. Ptolemy enumerated more than fifty of them[1]: by the year 400 all or nearly all of these had gathered themselves into a few great hordes or associations of tribes, (which may themselves be called overgrown tribes,) bearing severally the names of the Saxons, the Salian Franks, the Ripuarian Franks, the Angli, the Alamanni, the Burgundians, the Visigoths, the Ostrogoths, the Lombards. After 400 A.D. came the great migrations of the German peoples: some of them invaded the provinces of the Western Roman Empire, still full of wealth and of such civilisation as the Romans had planted there: others, in the second half of the fifth century, betook themselves to Britain, from whence the Romans had departed in the year 407.

During the eleven centuries which intervened between the migrations of the Germans and the year 1500, the Germans who went to Britain, Spain and Gaul succeeded in forming certain large political communities which are usually known as the nations of medieval Europe. These political communities as they existed about the year 1480 or 1500 possessed three of the distinguishing features of nations: for each of them was of large size, lived under a single government, and was composed of men well suited for living together and under one government: but all of them lacked one quality which is essential for the making of a perfect nation: and that lacking quality was a strong cohesion between the inhabitants of the different parts of their territories. But it will be necessary to observe in detail the processes by which the large political communities were built up.

The Saxons, Angles, and Jutes who went to Britain established themselves at first in a number of small settlements on its southern and eastern coasts. From these settlements they gradually pushed their way inland, and by 577 A.D. they had conquered nearly all the richest and most fertile regions in Britain. The many political communities formed by settlement and conquest were soon afterwards engaged in strife with one another: in the beginning of the ninth century the West Saxons

---

[1] Smith's *Atlas of Ancient Geography*, Map 13, contains a map of Germania Magna according to Ptolemy.

overpowered all their opponents and the West Saxon king received the submission of all the German settlers in the island. The conquering West Saxons and the conquered Angles and Jutes showed the same genius for amalgamation as had been shown by their forefathers in Germany long before: and by the middle of the ninth century all the Germans in Britain (we may now call them the English) had combined into a single large political community. Three times over, in 867–878, 988–1016, and 1066–1070, the English were disturbed by invasions of fresh immigrants from the continent of Europe: but on each occasion the new comers were successfully united in a single political community with the older settlers, and by the year 1174 or at any rate by 1215 the English people had been for the last time fashioned into one kindred under one government.

The German peoples who invaded Spain were the Vandals, the Alans, the Suevi and the Visigoths. The Visigoths proved to be the strongest of the four, and by the early years of the sixth century they had occupied nearly all the peninsula except the north east corner, which they left to the Suevi. In the enjoyment of the luxuries afforded by Roman civilisation, and in the fancied security of their position, they neglected the arts of war in which they had once so greatly excelled. In 710 A.D. their country was invaded and in the three following years was conquered by Moors from Africa, so that none of it was left to the Goths, the Suevi and some other tribes who were neither Germans nor Moors, except some valleys among the Pyrenees and a narrow strip of land about twenty miles broad and two hundred miles long between the shore of the Bay of Biscay and the mountain range of Cantabria and Asturias[1].

During the five centuries which followed the Moorish conquest of Spain the Goths who lived on the shores of the Bay of Biscay and the inhabitants of the southern valleys of the Pyrenees gradually expanded by reconquering territory from the Moors, and before the middle of the twelfth century had formed the two large political communities of Castile and

[1] Spruner-Menke, *Historischer Hand-Atlas*, *Maps* 14 and 15.

Arragon[1]. Each of these communities during its long contest with the Moors had acquired habits, thoughts and institutions of its own, and they were but little inclined to join themselves together into a single nation. The marriage of Ferdinand of Arragon with Isabella of Castile in 1469 produced as its result some time later that both Castile and Arragon were ruled by the same government: but differences and jealousies between the two peoples continued to exist long afterwards, even so late as the War of the Spanish Succession in the eighteenth century[2], and it may well be doubted whether the two were ever welded together into a single Spanish nation until after the terrible misfortunes which they endured and the great efforts which they made in a common cause during their war against Napoleon.

In Gaul the formation of a large political community was delayed till late in the middle ages; in Germany, the original home of the Germans, no large political community of great importance was established till late in the seventeenth century. In both countries the same hindrances stood in the way of the making of great communities. The two countries were included in the heterogeneous empires founded between 687 A.D. and 800 A.D. by the house of Pepin, especially by Charlemagne, the greatest man of the house of Pepin: in that empire, as in all heterogeneous empires, it was found necessary that the central ruler should delegate very great powers to the officials who governed provinces or districts: and under the circumstances of the time it was also found convenient for him to grant large estates of land to men who had been useful to him and could be trusted to serve him well in the future. In 843 Gaul (or the land of the West Franks) was severed from the empire, and set up a king of its own, who pretended to have the same powers as Charlemagne had exercised. But the kings of the West Franks could not control the local officials and landowners: by the eleventh century the local officials and the landowners had converted themselves into independent sovereigns, each ruling his own

---

[1] Hallam, *Middle Ages*, Chapter IV.
[2] Stanhope, *Reign of Queen Anne*, Vol. I. p. 264.

lands and the men who lived on his lands: that particular landowner who still enjoyed the title of king had no authority (or at any rate no authority which he could habitually exercise) except within the lands which specially belonged to him: and even within his own lands he, like the other landowners in Gaul, found that his authority was often disputed in arms by his tenants.

In the early years of the twelfth century Louis VI., owning or claiming to own an estate or demesne of land which had Paris as its centre and measured about 140 miles from north to south and about 50 miles from east to west, set himself to establish order and government within his demesne by force of arms. The inhabitants of the demesne valued the good government and the order that was maintained among them by Louis VI. and his grandson Philip II., and when the twelfth century ended they may be counted as forming a small political community or a body of men, possessing not only a common government, but also common interests habits and wishes[1]. In the thirteenth century the king's demesne was increased by the acquisition of Normandy, Anjou, Maine, Touraine, Poitou, Champagne in the north of Gaul, and by the distant region of Languedoc in the south. The new parts of the demesne were placed under the same government with the old, and no doubt those of them which lay together in the north of Gaul constantly tended to unite themselves into a single political community. But the work of unification was greatly impeded by causes all closely connected with the independence which the different parts of Gaul had possessed in the tenth and eleventh centuries, and it had not made very great progress in 1415 when France was invaded by the armies of the English. After the expulsion of the invaders the work was taken up again and carried on with better success by Charles VII., Louis XI. and the later kings of France.

In Germany events followed much the same course as in

---

[1] My statements about Frankish and early French history down to the reign of Philip II. are all based on original authorities: but see Kitchin, *History of France*, Vol. I., and some excellent maps (No. 57) in Droysen, *Historischer Hand-Atlas*.

Gaul; but they occurred later. The extinction of the Emperor's authority and the rise of the local governors and landowners to independence did not come to pass in Germany till the middle of the thirteenth century; and none of the princes who then gained their independence succeeded during the middle ages in rising to preeminence above the rest.

In order to complete our survey of the chief political communities of the middle ages we must glance at northern Italy and Switzerland. Northern Italy contained many important towns which had been founded by the Romans: during the early part of the middle ages it became the commercial centre of Europe: the towns grew in wealth and influence, and before the year 1200 they succeeded in making themselves independent, and constituted themselves as city states, resembling the city states of ancient Greece. In Switzerland three tribes of mountaineers in Uri, Schwyz and Unterwalden, in 1291, agreed to form a league or permanent alliance, which was afterwards joined by many of their neighbours, though no steps towards forming a federal state were taken till about the year 1500[1].

It has been remarked already that the large political communities of the middle ages were not thoroughly coherent or consolidated. A want of coherence was exhibited both in France and in England by the frequent recurrence of rebellions or civil strife, in France under John II. and Charles VI., in England under Edward II., Richard II. and Henry VI.; still more clearly was it made visible in France in 1356–1360 and 1415–1422 by the inability of the French to act unitedly in resistance to an invading enemy, and by the ease with which portions of French territory were detached from the dominions of the French king and transferred to the victorious invaders. The danger of civil discord was great enough in the fifteenth

---

[1] Oechsli, *Quellenbuch zur Schweizergeschichte*, pages 49, 199-202, 261-266. The second of these passages, especially page 200, proves that so late as 1481 no Swiss Federation had been made, but each canton was an independent state, managing its foreign relations for itself: the third shows that by 1512 a central body had been established which received ambassadors sent by foreign powers to the Swiss, and settled what answers the Swiss League should give them.

century when it arose mainly from the armies of retainers kept by ambitious noblemen: but it became still greater in the sixteenth, when differences of creed divided each people into two hostile camps. The disruptive forces at length became so strong that both France and England seemed to be in danger of losing the character of political communities and of lapsing into masses of heterogeneous elements; and accordingly each country adopted that kind of government which is best suited to hold heterogeneous elements together, namely, a monarchy with almost unlimited power. The subsequent histories of the two countries, though dissimilar in general character, were in one respect alike: in both countries civil war actually occurred, in France in the sixteenth century, in England in the seventeenth; and in each country experience of the miseries of war brought a love for the blessings of peace, with the result that France from 1700 to 1789 and England from 1745 to this day present very perfect examples of united nations.

Besides the nations of France, England, Spain, Scotland, Sweden, Norway and Denmark which grew up directly from the large political communities of the middle ages, others have been founded in more recent times, some of them having only a single government, and being therefore called unitary states, and others having one government for some purposes and many governments for other purposes, and being known as federal states. Among the unitary or non-federal nations we must notice Brandenburg-Prussia 1700–1866, Italy since 1859, Belgium, Holland, Greece, and the Balkan States: among the federal nations the United States of America and modern Switzerland stand out conspicuously. The German Empire founded in 1871 is a federal nation, though it differs from other federal nations because Prussia, one of its component states, is larger than all the other component states put together: Austria Hungary was for centuries a mere heterogeneous empire, but in recent times its parts have been held together by the possession of common interests and not by force, so that it has acquired some of the characters of a federation, though it cannot be said that it has grown together into a single nation.

But the making and consolidation of nations is not the only

kind of state-building that has gone on since the end of the middle ages: for other sorts of construction have also been actively carried on, and they have resulted in the making of a number of states that are larger than nations. In some cases two European nations or a European nation and some other European population have been brought under a single government: in other cases a European nation has expanded by the foundation of colonies far away from its original abode: and yet again in some cases a European state has conquered a host of non-European peoples and formed them into a heterogeneous empire dependent on itself.

The most conspicuous instances of the union of a nation with another nation or people occurred in 1683 when Alsace was acquired by France, in 1707 when England and Scotland placed themselves under one government, in 1771, 1793 and 1795 when parts of Poland were annexed to Prussia, and in 1801 when the United Kingdom of Great Britain and Ireland was formed. The enlarged states which result from such unions can never be strictly called single nations immediately after the union has taken place, and for a time at least after the union they must be denoted merely as unitary states: but usually they have not for most purposes differed very greatly from nations: for in all cases one of the two peoples united together has been a large and well consolidated nation and the other has been much smaller and far less perfectly organized: and consequently the larger partner in the union has had a predominant share in the government, and has gradually succeeded in communicating its own national characteristics and feelings to some part at least of the population of the lesser partner in the union.

A state formed by colonial expansion presents difficulties to any one who tries to define its nature. It is like a family of plants all sprung from one stock; the stock has sent out offshoots, which have themselves struck root, but are still connected with the parent stock from which they sprang. In one sense such an expanded state is still a single political community: in another sense each of the colonies which belongs to it is also a political community, though it never possesses complete independence, and therefore is not to be counted as a state.

The greatest conquerors of distant lands outside Europe have been the Spaniards, the English and the Russians. Their conquests formed three great political aggregates or heterogeneous empires, the Spanish Empire in southern and central America, the Indian Empire, and the Russian Empire. The Indian and the Russian Empires are administered by methods more or less resembling those used in the old heterogeneous Empire of the Romans by Constantine the Great and his successors: the administration of the Spaniards was very defective from the outset, and at the beginning of the nineteenth century their empire broke up into a number of independent states.

And now I may attempt a classification of all the more important forms that have been assumed by groups or collections of men living under governments. First of all, some of these groups are mere political aggregates, having little in common save the fact of living under one government, and the rest are political communities whose members have much else beside government in common. The mere aggregates will not need to be further divided; they are all heterogeneous empires held together by force. The political communities must be divided into three classes, tribes, cities, and the larger political communities. The class tribes needs no subdivision: cities must be divided according as they are inexpansive or expansive: the larger political communities (a class identical with the nations and those communities which possess many of the qualities of nations) need be subdivided only into unitary states or large political communities each with a single government only, and federal states or large political communities in which there is one government for some purposes and many governments for other purposes.

The essentials of a perfect classification are four in number. Firstly, it ought to be exhaustive or to comprehend all individual specimens, so that no individual shall be without a place in it. Secondly, the marks which distinguish the classes should be easily recognisable. Thirdly, the marks of one class should never be present in a single individual together with the marks of another: for, if they are, the individual is in two classes at once. Fourthly (and this is most essential of all), the classes should be such that many important general propositions are true of all the individuals which compose any given class.

It will be well to try to ascertain in what measure these essentials are found in a classification of European bodies politic under the five heads of tribes, cities, nations unitary and federal, and heterogeneous empires. Firstly, the classification is, I believe, so far exhaustive that it includes all those bodies which most clearly deserve to be called both political and European: it does not however provide a place for mere feudal principalities which never grew into nations, nor is it intended to include the Asiatic Empire of the Turks in Europe. Secondly, the marks which distinguish the classes are easily recognisable. Thirdly, the classification is decidedly imperfect because it does not make it impossible for a political body to be in two classes at once. But the possibility that a political body may be in two classes at once does not occur except during those periods when a community is gradually growing out of one form and into another. Such periods of transition have occurred in the history of many peoples: there was one in Greek history when the tribes were growing into cities: one in Roman history when the Republic was ceasing to be a mere enlarged city and was growing into a heterogeneous empire: and one in English history when the English were losing the character of a tribe and acquiring the qualities of a nation. But such periods of transition do not occur in the life of all peoples, and where they do occur, they are not usually of long duration when compared with the whole of the people's history. Fourthly, there are many important general propositions which are true of all or of nearly all the individuals in any given class. To establish such general propositions by historical evidence will be my task in the present chapters and in any future additions which I may be able to make to them. Some of these general propositions may be at once indicated in an imperfect form, though the proofs of them must be postponed.

The most important of these propositions are those which

assert that there is an intimate connexion between the form of a political body and the form of government by which it is ruled: and that each of the forms that a political body can assume has a certain type or certain types of government commonly and almost uniformly associated with it. The propositions may be set down in the following way. Firstly, all the tribes of which we have any good records have had governments not differing from one another in any important particular. Secondly, cities pure and simple or inexpansive cities have usually three kinds of government only, pure oligarchy, or pure despotism, or direct and almost unmixed democracy: and Republican Rome, the single example of an expanded city, had a government peculiar to itself. Thirdly, in the large unitary states or nations, it is, roughly speaking, true that three kinds of government have succeeded one another in regular sequence: at first, during the middle ages, they were under governments in which power belonged partly to a king and partly to an assembly of estates, the assembly consisting usually of the nobles, the prelates of the church, and representatives from rural districts and towns: afterwards, when they were in danger of disruption, they placed themselves under monarchies of unlimited or almost unlimited power, and these monarchies usually continued to exist after all danger of disruption had been removed: and now, in modern times, all unitary states are ruled by cabinets under the control or supervision of popular representative assemblies. Turning to federal states, which form the fourth class of political communities, we find that all of them are alike in having a central government both legislative and executive, whose sphere of action is strictly limited by the constitution to certain portions of the work of governing, and in permitting each of the states, which are joined together in the federation, also to have a government of its own, which controls all business except that portion which is allotted by the constitution to the central government of the federation. And, lastly, heterogeneous empires must, unless they are to break in pieces, have governments whose chief object is centralisation. Supreme power may belong to a despotic monarch or to a small body of men appointed by a foreign state which rules the empire: but in all cases the one thing necessary is that there shall be a central supreme power and that the commands of that supreme power shall be implicitly obeyed by everyone within the empire.

It will be observed that most of the propositions which I have enumerated are qualified with a saving word or saving clause to admit the existence of exceptions. The exceptions however are not, so far as I can judge, very numerous. Among the governments of city states the Cleisthenean constitution at Athens was exceptional, since, though it was more like a democracy than anything else, it was not by any means an unmixed democracy: and some similar exceptions occur, I believe, in the earliest part of the history of some medieval cities in Lombardy. During the middle ages, it was only in those peoples which best deserved the name of large political communities or incipient nations that an effective division of power between a king and an assembly of estates was to be found, and even in them it was not maintained without occasional interruptions: in England for example there were three periods (1258-1259, 1310-1322, and 1388-1389) of pure oligarchy, and two (1200-1215, and 1397-1399) of pure despotism: among the French and in some other peoples which had not truly acquired the character of political communities, we find a semblance of a division of power, but not the reality. The assertion that the nations during the sixteenth and seventeenth centuries were ruled by strong monarchical governments scarcely needs any qualification: there is however a short exceptional period in English history, 1649-1653, when the government was an oligarchy; and Poland never acquired a strong monarchical government, but was punished for the absence of such a government by ceasing to exist. In the course of the French Revolution 1789-1795 there occur some seeming exceptions to the propositions about forms of government which have been enumerated: but I believe they will be found not to be exceptions, if we observe that during those years Paris was practically an independent city state.

CHAPTER III.

GREEK POLITICAL INSTITUTIONS. HEROIC MONARCHIES.

THE political institutions of the Greeks will be examined first, because the Greeks are known to us at an earlier period than any other European people.

Hellas, the land of the Greeks, is about equal in size to half of Scotland or Ireland or to a third of England[1]. It is intersected by a network of continuous mountain ranges, which cannot be crossed without difficulty, and these ranges are almost everywhere so near together that it is impossible to travel more than twenty miles in any direction without crossing one of them. There are therefore no plains of any considerable extent, and the country is cut up into very numerous small areas, each enclosed, except towards the sea, within natural barriers which make egress and entrance alike difficult. These areas are of varying minuteness: by far the greater number of them measure only ten miles by ten, or twenty by five, but a few are of larger dimensions, and, in particular, Argolis contains about four hundred and fifty square miles, and is as large as Bedfordshire, Attica contains seven hundred and twenty, and just equals Berkshire, and Laconia, with about nine hundred, is of the same size as Warwickshire[2].

[1] In making this statement I have regarded Thessaly as not forming part of Hellas. Thessaly was completely cut off from the rest by two great ranges of mountains and was conquered before the beginning of Greek history by a people who were not truly Hellenic.

[2] These areas of Argolis, Attica, Laconia are calculated from the maps in Smith's *Atlas*: the other areas referred to are taken from the *Statesman's Yearbook*, or the article *Graecia* in Smith's *Dictionary of Geography*.

If communication by land is difficult, by sea it is easy, and was easy even in the earliest times. Greece and its islands have as much sea-board as any equal area in Europe; most of the natural divisions of the country have their share of coast with sheltered beaches where the boats or small ships of ancient times could be drawn up in safety: the Mediterranean, though it is sometimes as dangerous as any sea, is often calm: and by the age of Homer it had come to be a great highway for war, piracy and commerce.

The career of all the Greek communities, except Sparta, divides itself readily into periods. The first period, lasting till perhaps 700 B.C. or 650 B.C., was the period of tribes and tribal governments: the second, lasting to 338 B.C., was the period of cities and city governments. The period of the cities must however be divided into three lesser periods, each characterised by the prevalence of a certain kind of city government: the first of these lesser periods lasted from about 700 B.C. to 600 B.C., the second from 600 B.C. to 500 B.C., and the third from 500 B.C. to 338 B.C. Between 700 B.C. and 600 B.C. Athens, Corinth and Megara were under the domination of groups of privileged families, and many Greek cities in Sicily were also governed by small groups of citizens distinguished either by birth or by wealth: and, since the rule of a few is known as an aristocracy if the few rulers are the men best qualified to rule and if they use their power for the good of the whole community, but as an oligarchy if the few rulers govern for their own selfish interest, the century may be called the period of the early aristocracies and oligarchies. Between 600 B.C. and 500 B.C. nearly every Greek city, both in Greece proper and elsewhere, came under the rule of a τύραννος or usurper of absolute power, so that the century may be called the age of the tyrants or usurpers. And lastly, between 500 B.C. and 338 B.C. in many of the Greek cities a system of government was set up under which the whole body of the citizens acting collectively conducted the work of government, or at least all parts of it which can in the nature of things be conducted by a numerous assembly, while in other cities a small body of the richest citizens ruled selfishly for their own advantage and the advantage of their class; and, since any system in which the whole body of citizens directly conduct the work of government or the greater part of the work of government is known as a democracy, while the selfish rule of a few is, as we have seen, called an oligarchy, the period may best be called the age of the democracies and of the later oligarchies.

The Spartans were unlike, in their history their institutions and the aims of their policy, not only to all other Greek communities but perhaps to every other community that has ever existed: they never completely grew out of their tribal condition, never entirely abandoned their tribal government, and never formed themselves into a city like the other Greek cities: and besides all this they were in so many ways unlike to the rest of mankind that it will be necessary for me to speak of them by themselves and apart from the rest of the Greeks.

The Greek communities and their political systems from the earliest times to the first overthrow of Greek independence in 338 B.C. will be treated in the present and the next two chapters in the following order: firstly, we shall examine the tribes and the tribal governments, secondly, the institutions and government of the Spartans, and thirdly, the cities and the city-governments.

THE GREEK TRIBES AND TRIBAL GOVERNMENTS.

The numerous tribes which composed the Greek race ranged themselves in several groups, distinguished from one another in name, characteristics and fortunes. Among these groups the Achæans, the Dorians and the Ionians are historically the most important. The Achæan group includes all the tribes that are conspicuous in the Iliad and Odyssey: and from this circumstance it may safely be inferred that, when those poems were composed, the Achæan tribes had made more progress than any other Greeks in knowledge and political organisation. The Dorians in the days of Homer were an obscure tribe living in a little mountain valley of Northern Greece: in the next age they invaded the Peloponnesus, expelled the Achæans from their homes, and formed themselves into the four peoples of the Spartans, the Messenians, the Corinthians and the Argives. The Ionian tribes, the Athenians and twelve of the Greek cities of Asia Minor, including Miletus and Ephesus, were even later than the Dorian peoples in rising to importance. I shall deal first with the Achæans and then with the Dorians and Ionians.

1. *The Achæan tribes in the heroic age.*

When the Iliad and the Odyssey were composed the Achæans had formed a great number of small independent communities, some inhabiting islands, and others living in valleys surrounded by chains of mountains. The only tribe whose methods of government are depicted in some detail was one of the least of the Greek peoples, and had its home in Ithaca, a rocky island of the Ionian sea about seventeen miles long and three or four miles broad. The larger tribes were the Mycenæans, the Spartans, and the Achæans of Phthiotis. All the Achæan tribes were much alike in their political institutions: for the same political terms ($\beta\alpha\sigma\iota\lambda\epsilon\dot{\upsilon}\varsigma$, $\dot{\alpha}\gamma o\rho\dot{\eta}$, $\gamma\dot{\epsilon}\rho o\nu\tau\epsilon\varsigma$, $\lambda\alpha o\dot{\iota}$) are used in reference to the various tribes without distinction. Their governments were tribal in character, and we may call them either by the generic name of tribal governments, or by the name, which they more usually bear, of heroic monarchies.

The government of an Achæan tribe was conducted, in time of peace, in assemblies ($\dot{\alpha}\gamma o\rho\alpha\dot{\iota}$). The purposes for which they met included the announcement of any important news[1], discussion of any public business or question of policy[2] or the settlement of a litigation[3]. Our knowledge of their character and proceedings is derived from a full description in the second book of the Odyssey of an assembly held at Ithaca, and a shorter description in the Iliad[4].

Whenever the king desired that an assembly should be held he gave the heralds orders to require the immediate attendance

[1] *Odyssey* II. 30 ἀγγελίην στρατοῦ ἐρχομένοιο (news of the host returning).
[2] *Odyssey* II. 32 ἠέ τι δήμιον ἄλλο πιφαύσκεται ἠδ᾽ ἀγορεύει; (or has he any other public business to discuss?)
[3] *Iliad* XVIII. 497 νεῖκος (a dispute).
[4] *Odyssey* II. 1–259, *Iliad* XVIII. 497–508.

of the elders and the people[1]. The place of meeting was an open space in the city set apart for the purpose. In the midst was a circle of stone seats for the king and the elders[2], and one of the seats belonged specially to the king[3]: outside were the people, all of whom were compelled by the heralds to seat themselves on the ground[4] and to be silent[5]. When this had been done, the work of the assembly began; the speakers were the king and the elders, and the people either kept silence or perhaps indicated their approval by shouting or their dissent by murmurs. The councillors who sat with the king and had the right of speaking were for the most part (as the name γέροντες, if taken literally, denotes) men of age and experience: but younger men of good family, such as the wooers of Penelope[6], were also sometimes present among them and shared their privileges.

The assembly at Ithaca was irregularly summoned. The words of the first speaker, the aged Ægyptius, show that according to custom the king alone had the prerogative of issuing a summons by the voice of the heralds. Odysseus had been absent for twenty years: and Ægyptius says, "Since the godlike Odysseus departed in his hollow ships our assembly and

---

[1] *Odyssey* II. 6. The Ithacan assembly was summoned by the king's son in his father's absence: but the summons was irregular, as is shown in the next paragraph.

[2] *Iliad* XVIII. 503
οἵ δὲ γέροντες
εἵατ' ἐπὶ ξεστοῖσι λίθοις ἱερῷ ἐνὶ κύκλῳ.

The stone seats are mentioned only in the description of a judicial assembly: but all assemblies met, there is no doubt, in the same place.

[3] *Odyssey* II. 14 ἕζετο δ' ἐν πατρὸς θώκῳ (Τηλέμαχος), εἶξαν δὲ γέροντες (and Telemachus sat down in his father's seat, and the elders made way for him).

[4] See Grote's note in his *History*, Part I. ch. xx. His instances (*Iliad* II. 96 and *Iliad* XVIII. 246) are both taken from time of war: but it is not in the least likely that this detail was peculiar to assemblies held at such times.

[5] *Iliad* II. 96
ἐννέα δέ σφεας
κήρυκες βοόωντες ἐρήτυον, εἴ ποτ' ἀϋτῆς
σχοίατ' ἀκούσειαν δὲ διοτρεφέων βασιλήων

(and nine heralds were calling them to order, to stop clamouring and hearken to the heaven-born kings).

[6] At the Ithacan assembly the suitors Antinous, Eurymachus, and Leiocritus were among the speakers. *Odyssey* II. 84–254.

session has never been held. And now who is he that summoned us? who was compelled by so great necessity? has he heard news of our warriors coming back, and hastens to tell us? or has he aught else of our country's weal to speak about? I say he is a good man, God bless him! and may Zeus perform for him whatever his heart desires![1]"

The business of the assembly at Ithaca was not exactly judicial and can scarcely be described as deliberation on policy. Telemachus summoned the elders and the people in order to declare to them that the proceedings of the suitors were intolerable to him, that he bade them leave his house, that he would resist them by force, if he could, and that if they were slain in his house no price for their lives would be due from him to their kindred.

The assembly came to no formal resolution: the practical result of it was settled by the speeches of the elders without any intervention of the common folk, and was expressed by the last speaker Leiocritus, who declared that the suitors were not afraid of Telemachus nor of Odysseus himself, and bade all those who were present to go away each about his own business.

An assembly occupied in administering justice was depicted in a compartment of the shield of Achilles, which the poet thus describes[2]: "A people too was there, gathered in assembly: and in their midst a dispute had arisen, and two men were disputing about the price (wergild) of a man that had been slain. The one was declaring aloud to the multitude that he had paid the whole, the other that he had received none of it. And both were ready to go before a judge to get a decision: and the people on this side and on that were cheering them on, but were restrained by the heralds. And there sat the elders on seats of wrought stone in a circle protected by the gods, holding staves given them by the loud-voiced heralds; and then the elders were arising in turn to give judgement. And in the midst were lying two talents of gold to be given to him whose judgement was the straightest[3]."

In this assembly, as in the other, power belonged solely to

---

[1] *Odyssey* II. 25-34.   [2] *Iliad* XVIII. 497-508.
[3] *Or perhaps*, to him who best proved his case.

those who formed the inner circle. The presence of the king in the judicial assembly is not mentioned, but kings did sometimes take part in giving dooms, for Nestor says to Agamemnon: "O most famous son of Atreus, Agamemnon, king of men, thou shalt be my ending and thou my beginning, because thou art king of many people and Zeus has given thee the sceptre *and judgements* that thou mayst be their counsellor[1]."

There is a story in the Odyssey which indicates more clearly than the descriptions of the assemblies that, in time of peace, supreme power belonged to the king and the elders jointly and not to the king alone or to the elders alone. While Laertes was reigning in Ithaca three hundred sheep belonging to Ithacans were stolen by robbers from Messenia. Odysseus, the king's son, was sent to ask satisfaction for the wrong: and it is expressly stated that it was the king and the other elders who empowered him to act as ambassador[2].

In time of war the king had supreme and exclusive command over his tribe. Thus when Achilles king of the Phthiotians was angry with Agamemnon, he was able without consultation with any one to withdraw the whole Phthiotian contingent from aiding in the war against the Trojans: and, when he began to relent, nothing was needed but a word from him to place his forces in the field again under the orders of his friend Patroclus[3]. Agamemnon on the other hand, being the commander of a host composed of contingents from many tribes, found it necessary, before issuing any orders to the whole army, to consult the kings who were taking part with him in his enterprise[4].

Our conclusions about the political system which prevailed in the Greek tribes of the heroic age can be shortly summed up. In time of peace all public business was conducted in assemblies: in these assemblies the king and the elders alone

---

[1] *Iliad* IX. 96–99. [2] *Odyssey* XXI. 16–21.

[3] *Iliad* XVI. 38–39. Patroclus says to him, "If thou art deterred by some divine command from fighting thyself, yet let me go and give me thy people, the Myrmidons (i.e. the Phthiotians)": and Achilles (lines 49-65) replies, "I have been wronged and therefore will not fight: thou shalt wear my armour and command the Myrmidons."

[4] *Iliad* II. 53, IX. 9–17, 89–95.

had the right of speaking, and the king was expected to act according to the advice of the elders. In time of war the king was commander-in-chief, and could act without control from any one.

Besides the political institutions of the ancient Greeks, some of the general conditions of their life may be noticed. They depended for their subsistence partly on their cattle and partly on the produce of the ground, and most of the poorer free men, not possessing slaves, lived in the country to tend their herds and till their lands. Some, who had no herds and no lands of their own, worked as labourers for hire[1]. The estates and the cattle of the kings and rich men were committed to the charge of slaves captured in war or in freebooting expeditions[2]. The kings and rich men themselves lived, not scattered over the open country after the fashion of the Germans described by Tacitus[3], but collected in cities. Thus at Ithaca the house of the king and the houses of the wooers of Penelope were all close together: for at the end of the first day in the story of the Odyssey the wooers "went each to his house to sleep[4]" and on the morrow at the dawn of day at the summons of the heralds they "came very quickly to the assembly[5]": Pylos, where Nestor lived, is called the gathering place and the abodes of the Pylians[6]: and, not to multiply instances, words denoting cities are regularly applied in the Homeric poems to the dwelling-places of the heroes.

The cities of the heroic age had, for their defence, in all cases a fortress or strong place of refuge close at hand, and some of them at least were entirely encircled with a wall. Argos lay at the foot of the steep isolated mountain of the Larissa which rose about a thousand feet above it: Corinth was under the still loftier Acrocorinthus; Mycenæ and Athens had

---

[1] *Odyssey* XI. 489 θητευέμεν.

[2] Grote's *Greece*, octavo edition vol. I. p. 487, cabinet edition vol. II. p. 98.

[3] Tac. *Germ.* 16. Nullas Germanorum populis urbes habitari satis notum est, ne pati quidem inter se junctas sedes. Colunt discreti ac diversi, ut fons, ut campus, ut nemus placuit.

[4] *Odyssey* I. 424 κακκείοντες ἔβαν οἰκόνδε ἕκαστος.

[5] *Odyssey* II. 8 τοὶ δ' ἠγείροντο μάλ' ὦκα.

[6] *Odyssey* III. 31 Πυλίων ἀνδρῶν ἀγυρίν τε καὶ ἕδρας.

each its Acropolis, a strong fortress built on a rock rising abruptly but to no great height above the town. That in some cases the lower city, as distinct from the Acropolis, had also its own outer wall is proved by the whole story of the siege of Troy, which shows that cities entirely enclosed in fortifications were well known to Homer[1].

There are numberless passages in the Iliad and Odyssey which prove that the houses of the heroes were well stored with wealth. The suitors who intruded as guests at the house of Telemachus always found plenty of cattle, bread, wine and oil ready at hand for their riotous feasts, and yet Telemachus was but a poor man among the Greek princes. When Telemachus paid a visit to Menelaus and Helen at Sparta he was astonished to find that their palace glittered with gold and silver, with electrum (a mixture of two metals) and with ivory[2]. The chamber of Odysseus at Ithaca contained abundance of gold and bronze, and clothing in chests and sweet smelling oil and wine in jars against his return[3]. The metal used for weapons was brass or bronze: agricultural implements were chiefly made of iron: of the precious metals gold was more commonly used than silver[4]. We do not hear that any of these metals were obtained in the heroic age from the soil of Greece itself, and may fairly conjecture that they were brought to the Greeks by the Phœnicians who in that age were more active in trade than any other people[5].

[1] Especially the scene of the death of Hector in the twenty-second book of the Iliad. Achilles having driven all the Trojans except Hector within their walls, pursued Hector thrice round the city, in the sight of the Trojans on the walls and of the host of the Greeks assembled on the plain outside the city. If any part of the city had been outside the wall, it must have been mentioned as impeding or aiding the flight of Hector, or as having been captured by the Greeks. As it is, the poet has no landmark outside the city to show how far the chase had extended except a fountain where the two springs, one hot and one cold, of the Scamander, had been built round with stone platforms on which clothing was washed by the Trojan women.

[2] *Odyssey* IV. 68–75.   [3] *Odyssey* II. 337–343.

[4] The evidence concerning the use of the metals is collected by Grote, octavo edition vol. I. p. 493, cabinet edition vol. II. pp. 104, 105.

[5] For the dealings of the Phœnicians see the story in which Eumæus the swineherd narrates how he was kidnapped as a child by Phœnician traders. *Odyssey* XV. 403–484.

The population of a city must have consisted of the wealthy families who had slaves to till their lands and tend their flocks and of those few artificers or professional men whose business brought them to live near the houses of the rich. Among the handicraftsmen were the carpenter, the copper-smith, the leather-dresser, the worker in gold: the professions were those of the leech, the prophet and the bard[1]. Thus it may be that in an assembly the people outside the sacred circle did not greatly surpass in number the elders who sat within it: for there were no classes to constitute a people except the younger members of the families of the elders and the few men who were induced to live in the city to find employment for their knowledge or skill.

2. *The Dorians and the Ionians in the heroic age.*

Before the beginning of Greek History, properly so called, the Achæan peoples, so important in the eyes of Homer, had sunk into comparative insignificance, and the first places in the Hellenic world had been filled by Dorians and Ionians. The original abode of the Dorians was a small mountainous country called Doris not far from Thermopylæ[2]. From hence bands of adventurers had gone forth and, invading Peloponnesus, had expelled the Achæans from Sparta, Messenia, Argos and Corinth, had occupied their territories and had copied their institutions. The Ionians in Attica had grown in prosperity and power, and, like the Dorian tribes, had adopted that form of government which I have called heroic monarchy.

Of the Dorian kingly government at Corinth we know nothing but its existence[3]: of the Messenian kings we have many stories told by Myron of Priene, but, on reading them side by side with the stories told by Geoffrey of Monmouth

---

[1] Grote, *Greece*, octavo edition vol. I. p. 486, cabinet edition vol. II. p. 97. For the worker in gold see *Odyssey* III. 425.

[2] Herodotus VIII. 31 in speaking of the position of Doris remarks, "This country is the mother country of the Dorians in Peloponnesus."

[3] Diodorus Siculus VII. fragment 9. Diodorus wrote about 20–10 B.C.

about King Arthur, I thought that for complete untrustworthiness there was nothing to choose between the two authors[1]: concerning the early kings of Argos Athens and Sparta, a few facts are established on good authority, and these I shall now proceed to state.

Argos, with its two neighbours Mycenæ and Tiryns, was in some respects unlike the other Greek communities. Elsewhere in Greece during the heroic age each community occupied the whole of a natural division of the country, and had its territory fenced round with natural barriers. In the Argolic plain three Achæan communities had found room to settle, exactly as in Italy many communities found room to settle in and around the plain of Latium: and thus the Argolic communities rather resembled the Latin cities than the Greek tribes. Their city walls were of exceptional strength, as the remains of them testify: their kings were richer and were exalted to a greater eminence above their subjects than the other Greek kings, for the palace of the king at Tiryns occupies nearly the whole of the upper citadel and is such as to demand a most prodigal expenditure of labour for its construction[2], and Agamemnon king of Mycenæ is represented by the poet of the Iliad as a powerful monarch. It cannot be doubted that the three cities had the same reasons for making their walls strong and their kings powerful as the Romans had in the days of Servius Tullius: they feared that they might be conquered by their neighbours, and hoped that they might themselves be the conquerors.

After the Dorian conquest the three cities still continued to exist: Argos was the strongest of them, but Mycenæ acted independently of Argos so late as the year 480 B.C. in sending a contingent to fight against the Persians at Thermopylæ[3]. The great power of the Dorian monarchy was conspicuous in the reign of Pheidon, who at some time between 750 B.C. and 600 B.C. became so powerful that he was able to conduct an

---

[1] Myron wrote about 220 B.C. His stories about the early Messenian kings are preserved by Pausanias in his fourth book.

[2] Professor Gardner, *New Chapters in Greek History*, pp. 96–101.

[3] Pausanias II. 16. 5.

expedition from his own city in the east of the Peloponnesus to Olympia in the west and to deprive the Eleians by force of their prerogative of presiding over the Olympic festival[1]. He also established a hegemony or lordship over a number of Greek peoples in the neighbourhood of Argos, which had long been independent. The tradition of his conquest says simply that he "recovered the whole lot of Têmenus which had been broken up into many parts[2]." Têmenus, according to the legends of the Heracleids, was one of the leaders of the Dorians in their invasion of the Peloponnesus: and it seems that his "lot" must have included the tribes that lived at Cleonæ, Phlius, Sicyon, Epidaurus, Trœzen, and Ægina. Pheidon's conquest of these tribes was a remarkable achievement, since all of them were protected against Argos by mountain ranges or by sea: and it gave him such despotic authority over his own subjects at Argos that he is counted among the τύραννοι[3]. But it seems that he ought not, strictly speaking, to be reckoned among them, being unlike to the rest of them in two important particulars: first, that his despotic authority at Argos was no doubt necessary in order to enable Argos to keep control over the dependent peoples, and second, that it is not likely that he ever incurred the hatred of the people of Argos: for, if he had been hated by his own subjects, his power outside Argos must have promptly come to an end. After his time the power of the king at Argos ceased to be despotic, the neighbouring tribes recovered their independence, and the monarchy sank into obscurity, though it continued to exist so

---

[1] Pausanias (VI. 22. 2) in speaking of this expedition assigns it to the eighth Olympiad or the year 748 B.C. I have not ventured to regard his date as trustworthy, because Professor Mahaffy (*Problems in Greek History*, Chapter III.) has shown reasons for doubting whether the order of the early Olympiads was correctly given in the lists which were current among the Greeks. His date however cannot well be earlier than 750 B.C., since it was after the Olympic festivals had become important: and it cannot be later than 600 B.C., because in that case clearer traditions about him would have been preserved.

[2] Ephorus, who wrote about 350 B.C., records this. His words are quoted by Grote, octavo edition vol. II. p. 90, cabinet edition vol. II. p. 316, from Strabo.

[3] Aristotle, *Politics* v. 10. 6, in Bekker's edition (Oxford, 1837). Welldon, p. 381. Pausanias VI. 22. 2.

late as 480 B.C. when Greece was invaded by the Persians under Xerxes[1].

In Attica we can carry back our view not only to the age of the heroic monarchy but to the age which preceded it. The country, though it is, as we have seen, of small extent, and though it is not traversed by any continuous ranges of mountains, was originally peopled by a number of independent communities, each contained within a single village or small township: and it is probable that these little communities retained their independence till after the time of Homer; for Athens, which rose to greatness by subjugating them, is rarely mentioned in the Homeric poems, and never, I believe, in any passage which belongs to the poems as they were originally composed. In course of time however a powerful king arose at Athens, who succeeded in bringing the whole country under a single monarchy of the heroic type: and Thucydides tells us that in his own days the union of Attica under Athens was regularly celebrated at a public festival[2].

The Spartans, instead of having one king, had two kings and two royal families[3], so that their system of government may best be described as a dual heroic kingship. Of this government, and of the conquests made by the Spartans while they lived under it, I shall have more to say in the next chapter.

Of the other tribes in the pre-historic age we have no traditions: but Thucydides[4] says without hesitation concerning the early Greeks in general that their governments were "hereditary kingly governments with limited prerogatives": and the same view, which was shared by all the later Greeks, falls in with the little that is known of the Greek peoples in the first two or three centuries of their history.

---

[1] The king of Argos in 480 B.C. is noticed by Herodotus (VII. 149).

[2] Thucydides II. 15. The original independence of the small communities is most fully vouched for by the festival, called τὰ συνοίκια, or the union of dwellings: and it furnishes a reason for the policy adopted by Cleisthenes of establishing popular local governments in the demes, or villages and townships, of Attica: see Chapter V.

[3] Herodotus VI. 52.

[4] Thucydides I. 13 ἐπὶ ῥητοῖς γέρασι πατρικαὶ βασιλεῖαι.

It is clear from many indications that the monarchical part of the old tribal constitutions was necessary or especially useful to the primitive Greek peoples so long as they were employed in making conquests or settlements of new territory, and no longer. In the prehistoric age the Athenians and all the Dorian peoples were conquering peoples: and all of them made their conquests under the leadership of kings. In the next age, which came between the heroic period and the beginning of Greek history in the proper sense of the word, the great majority of the Greek peoples had ceased to acquire new territory within Greece and had also ceased or were ceasing to be monarchically governed: two peoples, the Spartans and the Argives, were exceptional both in continuing to make territorial conquests and in still living under kingly rule.

CHAPTER IV.

SPARTA.

THE Spartans present so many peculiarities and are so unlike to any other people that I must divide what I have to say about them under separate heads. In regard to the Spartans before the Peloponnesian war I shall describe (I) their political surroundings, (II) their customs, (III) their constitution: for the period of the war and that which followed it, I shall give (IV) a general view of their commonwealth as it then stood.

I. The Spartans or Spartiatæ were the strongest and most warlike of those Dorian tribes who at some time after the time of Homer and yet long before the beginning of history migrated from the rocky valley of Doris in northern Greece and invaded the Peloponnesus. They subsequently lived in the unwalled city of Sparta as a small nation of conquerors surrounded by the two subject populations of the Periœci and the Helots, who peopled the country of Laconia. In 480 B.C., when the Spartans were at the height of their power, just after their king Leonidas and his three hundred had made their heroic defence at Thermopylæ, Xerxes asked Demaratus, who had once been king of Sparta but had been deposed, to tell him how many warriors remained to the Lacedæmonians and how many of them were as brave as the three hundred; Demaratus replied: "O king, the number of the Lacedæmonians is great and their cities are many: thou shalt know what thou desirest to learn. There is in Lacedæmon a city Sparta, of about eight thousand fighting men, and all these are like to those that fought at Thermopylæ: the other Lacedæmonians are not indeed equal to these, but yet they are brave¹." As the Spartans of military age numbered eight thousand we may reckon that forty thousand was about the number of persons, including women and children, who belonged to Spartan families and formed the Spartan nation.

The Periœci were "the other Lacedæmonians, not indeed equal to the Spartiatæ, but yet brave men," and by them the cities of Lacedæmon except Sparta were inhabited. It seems that the Periœci were decidedly more numerous than the Spartiatæ: in the year after the conversation between Xerxes and Demaratus the force, which was sent out to fight the Persian general Mardonius and which took part in the great battle of Platæa, consisted of five thousand Spartans, of thirty-five thousand light armed Helots, seven Helots being allotted as attendants to each Spartan, and of five thousand picked hoplites or heavy armed warriors from the Periœci². As these Periœci were picked men, there were more to pick from: of the force of Spartiatæ Grote remarks that "throughout the whole course of Grecian history we never hear of any number of Spartan citizens at all approaching to five thousand being put on foreign service at the same time³."

It is not certain whether the Periœci were Achæans or Dorians in origin. Whichever they were, our view of the Spartans and their government will be much the same. The Periœci were not treated with distrust or systematic cruelty: they retained their personal freedom under the Spartan rule, they continued to inhabit the towns or cities of Laconia, and in each of their towns to manage their local affairs for themselves⁴: but they had no voice whatever in the politics of Sparta, which were controlled exclusively by the Spartans.

---

¹ Herodotus VII. 234.
² Herodotus IX. 10, IX. 28, and IX. 11.
³ Grote, *Greece*, octavo edition vol. III. p. 404, cabinet edition vol. v. p. 11.
⁴ If they had not possessed the management of their local affairs, their communities would scarcely have been called πόλεις by Herodotus in the conversation between Xerxes and Demaratus. Herodotus VII. 234; Smith's *Dict. Antiq.* article Periœci.

Occasionally a man of ability from among the Periœci was promoted to a position of trust: thus in the year 412 B.C. a man named Deiniadas, a Periœcus, commanded a squadron of ships in the war on the coasts of Asia Minor and of Lesbos[1]. The Helots formed in the fifth century B.C. a large population of serfs who tilled the soil: they were the property of the Spartan state, which however placed the services of Helots at the disposal of the Spartans and Periœci for the cultivation of their estates. The Helots, who were bound to the soil on any given estate were compelled every year to render a fixed quantity of produce to the owner: on the residue they and their families subsisted[2].

The name εἵλωτες denotes captives taken in war[3]. It was believed by the Greeks that the Spartans, when first they made their conquest of Laconia, reduced some of those whom they conquered to the condition of Helots as above described: and the account given by them of the institutions of Lycurgus implies that the lawgiver foresaw some danger such as would arise from a large servile population. But if the Helots were dangerous in the age of Lycurgus, they became far more dangerous after the Spartans had conquered the Messenian country that lay to the west of Laconia and of the range of Taygetus. The Messenians were Dorians like the Spartans, and like them had conquered a large district of the Peloponnesus. Against these neighbours and kinsmen the Spartans waged two long wars, one probably in the eighth century B.C. and the other probably in the seventh[4]. In the second war they were completely successful, and at the end of it they

---

[1] Thucydides VIII. 22 ἦρχε τῶν νεῶν Δεινιάδας περίοικος (Deiniadas a Periœcus was in command of the ships).

[2] These statements about the condition of the Helots are not given by either Herodotus or Thucydides, but are found in Plutarch and Pausanias. Plutarch wrote about 60-70 A.D., and Pausanias about 170-180 A.D.: but both copied authors probably of the fourth century B.C. Pausanias (III. 20. 6) speaks of the Helots as slaves belonging to the state (δοῦλοι τοῦ κοινοῦ): the rest comes from Plutarch, *Lycurgus*, ch. 8.

[3] See Smith's *Dict. Antiq.*, third edition, article Helotes.

[4] The dates of the Messenian wars cannot be determined with certainty. See the note at the end of this chapter.

reduced the Messenians, who had for some two or three centuries been a free and independent Dorian people, to the condition of Helots[1]. But to hold the territory was almost as hard as to win it: and to keep the Messenians enslaved was almost as hard as to enslave them. The territory is separated from Laconia by a chain of mountains, and the new serfs were more dangerous than the original Helots because they remembered their freedom. From the time of the conquest of Messenia the little Spartan nation stood in perpetual danger of a great servile revolt. When, in 464 B.C., a rebellion of the Helots actually occurred, it imperilled the existence of the state. The Spartans at one time despaired of putting it down without external aid, and, when the Athenians offered them the services of an armed force, accepted the offer. Subsequently, when their jealousy of Athens revived and they resolved to rely on their own unaided efforts, they had to spend all their strength for nine years before they compelled the Helots in their stronghold on Mount Ithomê to capitulate on condition that they should depart from the Peloponnesus and never return[2]. Even after these brave men had gone into exile, there were plenty of Helots left to keep the Spartans in anxiety: and Thucydides in telling of the treacherous murder of the two thousand Helots in 424 B.C. remarks incidentally that "at all times most of the institutions of the Lacedæmonians were framed with a view to the Helots, to guard against their insurrections[3]."

II. The singular regulations under which the Spartans lived were designed to discipline all the males among their scanty numbers into a formidable military brotherhood. Possibly some of these regulations had already been established

---

[1] Pausanias (III. 20. 6) expressly says that those serfs who were acquired by the Spartans not in their original conquest of Laconia but subsequently (that is to say at the conquest of Messenia) were Messenian Dorians.

[2] The account of the revolt and its duration are taken from Thucydides I. 101–103. The date of its beginning is given by Pausanias IV. 24. 2 as being the seventy-ninth olympiad: i.e. seventy-eight times four years after 776 B.C.: i.e. 464 B.C.

[3] Thucydides IV. 80.

before they left their original abodes in Doris to migrate to the Peloponnesus: they were attributed to Lycurgus, a wise lawgiver, who is placed by the legends after the migration and some generations before the first Spartans of whom we have any historical knowledge: but the extreme strictness of their enforcement may have dated from the end of the second Messenian war, which reduced a whole people to servitude.

The earliest detailed account of the customs of the Spartans is given in a treatise on the Commonwealth of the Lacedæmonians, which has been attributed to Xenophon. Whoever the author may have been, it speaks of the Spartans as if they were almost irresistible in warfare: and hence it must be inferred that it was written before 371 B.C., when they suffered a severe and humiliating defeat at Leuctra in Bœotia. It gives a picture of Spartan customs whose chief outlines I shall try to reduce within the dimensions of a sketch.

The aim of the Spartan discipline was to ensure the greatest possible efficiency in the little band of warriors who formed the Spartan army. To this end it was first necessary that the race should be healthy: and as strong parents were likely to have strong offspring, the women no less than the men were trained in gymnastic exercises and contests[1]. The boys ceased at an early age to be under the sole authority of their own parents and were placed under the command of an officer of state whose title was παιδονόμος or warden of the boys[2], and were also compelled to obey any Spartan who had children of his own[3]. The training of the boys under their warden is not described in detail: but there is no doubt it consisted in gymnastics and in marching and dancing to music. The moral qualities which were insisted on were firstly personal courage and endurance, and secondly a modest demeanour in the young. The boys had to go barefoot, were allowed only one garment to wear throughout the year in heat and cold alike, and were kept on short rations of food: they were encouraged to steal

---

[1] [Xenophon] *De Rep. Lac.* 1. § 4.
[2] [Xenophon] *De Rep. Lac.* 2. § 2.
[3] [Xenophon] *De Rep. Lac.* 6. § 1, § 2.

food, but, if they were caught, were severely beaten for not having stolen cleverly[1]; and, if one of them complained to his father that another boy had beaten him, the father was thought to have disgraced himself if he did not give him a sound thrashing in addition[2]. The young men always walked silent with their eyes modestly fixed on the ground before them; and from this behaviour you could no more seduce them than you could a statue[3]. The great deference paid to age is merely hinted at in this treatise[4] but it is well known from other sources.

When the youths grew up to be men they were compelled to dine at the common meal provided for them: and unless they paid their contributions to its cost they lost the rights of citizenship. Their military training no doubt still continued: for the operations of warfare which the author describes were such as to require every man in the army to be always familiar with them from recent recollection[5]. Every Spartan was not only compelled to concentrate his attention on military excellence, but was completely cut off from all commercial pursuits and even from agriculture[6]. Commerce and all useful arts were left to the Periœci: the Spartan could practise none of them without degradation. His expenditure consisted in his contribution to the common meals and in the cost of maintaining a house for his wife and daughters and his sons till they were placed under the care of the warden of the boys. His income was derived from his lands which were tilled by Helots assigned to him by the State. The accumulation of wealth was severely discouraged: the possession of gold or silver was criminal and was punished with a fine: the currency was made of iron and was so cumbrous that no one could have much of it without the knowledge of all, since a quantity worth ten minæ (£40 sterling) would demand large storage-room and a waggon to remove it[7].

As every Spartan was a soldier all his life long from attain-

---

[1] All these details from [Xenophon] *De Rep. Lac.* 2.
[2] [Xenophon] *De Rep. Lac.* 6. § 2.
[3] [Xenophon] *De Rep. Lac.* 3.
[4] [Xenophon] *De Rep. Lac.* 9. § 5.
[5] [Xenophon] *De Rep. Lac.* 11.
[6] [Xenophon] *De Rep. Lac.* 7. § 1.
[7] [Xenophon] *De Rep. Lac.* 7. § 5.

ing manhood till he was too old for service, the organisation of the army must be counted among the important parts of the Spartan institutions. At a great battle fought and won by the Spartans in the year 418 B.C. the number of Spartiatæ on service was about three thousand one hundred. The force was divided into six regiments of five or six hundred men, each containing four smaller divisions, and sixteen smallest divisions or companies, which last bore the name of ἐνωμοτίαι, or bands of sworn soldiers. Each regiment had its commander and so had all its compartments down to the smallest: the commander gave his orders to the officers next below him, and they to the commanders of companies: and it was only from these last that the orders reached the soldiers[1]. The success of the whole system thus depended on the obedience of the lesser officers to their commander, and above all on the efficiency and good discipline of the companies or Enomoties.

The drill of each company was carried to the highest pitch of perfection: this at least is clear from the description of their evolutions given in the treatise from which I have so often quoted[2]. The number of men in a company seems to have been normally twenty-five, since two companies were sometimes called a fifty[3]: on some occasions it might be thirty-two or thirty-six. As it was usual at the beginning of a war to call out all the Spartans who were below a certain age[4], it is probable that none but men of the same age were placed together in a company, since in the absence of such an arrangement the proclamation of war might have divided each company into two parts, one part going to fight and the other staying at home. And if each company consisted of equals in age we may conjecture that when a Spartan attained the age of manhood he was immediately sworn in as a member of a company, and with that company he remained throughout his life unless he had to be drafted into another company to fill a vacancy.

[1] All this is from Thucydides v. 66 and v. 68.
[2] [Xenophon] *De Rep. Lac.* 11. The description takes up the second half of the chapter.
[3] Thus in [Xenophon] *De Rep. Lac.* 11 a commander of two companies is called πεντηκοστήρ or πεντηκοντήρ a captain of fifty.
[4] [Xenophon] *De Rep. Lac.* 11 : at the beginning of the chapter.

On the march one company led the way and the others followed in order. When an enemy came in sight, each regiment was able by means of evolutions of companies to form itself for battle in the dense array of the phalanx; and further by varying the evolutions the phalanx was made to face in any direction that was desired, and it was ensured that the front rank was composed entirely of the very best of the warriors[1].

The Spartan soldiers seem to have had no defensive armour except a large brazen shield: their dress was of a bright red[2] colour, and probably consisted of a single large plaid which could be fastened with a brooch at the shoulder[3]: for offensive weapons they had a long spear and short sword[4]. A regiment arranged in phalanx had a front rank of about sixty-four men as in the great battle in 418 B.C.: each of the ranks behind contained the same number, and there were in some cases as many as eight ranks[5]. For a body thus arranged the long spear for thrusting was obviously the best weapon: but the short sword was also needed whenever there was a close combat between man and man.

III. We have already seen[6] that the Spartans in prehistoric times lived under a system of government which I have called dual heroic kingship: their political institutions were in most respects the same as those of the other Greeks in the heroic age, but they regularly had two kings reigning at the same time, each being head by descent of one of the two royal houses. After the establishment of the dual heroic kingship but still in the prehistoric age the Spartans introduced further modifications in their system of government: and since their descendants, whether rightly or wrongly, believed that the wise lawgiver Lycurgus had been the author of these changes, the modified system of government is known as the constitution of

---

[1] [Xenophon] *De Rep. Lac.* 11. The description of the evolutions there given is well explained in Smith, *Dictionary of Antiquities*, third edition, vol. I. p. 770, under the word Exercitus.
[2] [Xenophon] *De Rep. Lac.* 11: at the beginning of the chapter, στολὴν φοινικίδα.
[3] Smith, *Dict. Ant.* third edition, article Tribon.
[4] Smith, *Dict. Ant.* third edition, vol. I. p. 773.
[5] Thucydides v. 68.
[6] See p. 35.

Lycurgus. This celebrated constitution is defined in a ῥήτρα or solemn compact said to have been dictated to Lycurgus by the Delphic priestess and accepted by the Spartans: Plutarch has preserved a document which professes to be the original text: and, though the pretensions of this document to extreme antiquity are probably unfounded, there is no doubt that it gives a truthful account of the government[1]. It orders Lycurgus "to found a temple of Zeus Syllanius and Athena Syllania, to divide the people into tribes (φυλαί) and obes (ὠβαί), to establish a senate of elders, thirty in number with the commanders (i.e. the kings), to hold assemblies at fixed times between Babyca and Knakion, and so to propose measures and take decisions on them: and that the commons (δᾶμος, δῆμος, the whole of the Spartiatæ) should have (? the decision?)[2] and authority." Thus the constitution of Lycurgus retained all the three component parts of the system to which I have given the name of dual kingship, the two kings, the council of elders, and the assembly of the people: but it prescribed that the meetings of the king and elders and people were to be held no longer according to the caprice of the kings but at fixed times and between two places which were both in the town of Sparta or close to it: the council of elders was to consist of exactly thirty members, the two kings being included in that number: and the assembly of the people was to possess authority (κράτος).

The powers that belonged severally to the kings to the elders and to the assembly are not defined. But the constitution was made in the age of the heroic monarchies and was derived from a dual heroic kingship by the introduction of

[1] Plutarch, *Lycurgus*, 6. The document, being in prose and not ambiguous, bears no resemblance to the genuine utterances of the Delphic priestess; and therefore I think not only that it is not an oracle really delivered to Lycurgus but also that it was not composed while the oracle of Delphi was active and the character of its utterances well known: that is to say, before 450 B.C. or 400 B.C. I imagine it to be the work of some antiquarian, who knew the Doric dialect extremely well: such a man might no doubt be found at Alexandria during or after the reign of Ptolemy Philadelphus B.C. 285-247: for Alexandria was then the home of all sorts of learning, and was the place in which, about the year 270 B.C., Theocritus the greatest of the Doric poets wrote the best of his Idylls.

[2] The text is uncertain here.

slight alterations. We may accordingly assume that in the system of Lycurgus, as in the government that preceded it, the important right of initiating measures was intended to belong exclusively to the kings and elders, and that the "authority" reserved to the popular assembly was no more than a right of voting Aye or No on proposals which the kings and elders submitted to it. In making this assumption we shall moreover be in agreement with Plutarch[1], who, either from such merely probable reasoning as we can use or on the authority of some writer who preceded him, states that the kings and elders alone had the initiative. In course of time however the assembly attempted to amend what was put before it or to initiate proposals of its own, and a second enactment ($\dot{\rho}\dot{\eta}\tau\rho\alpha$) was made to put a stop to its usurpations. From the stories of the wars with Messenia we learn that the command in war was one of the prerogatives of the kings.

The first historical Spartan is Theopompus, who was one of the two kings at some time between 750 B.C. and 650 B.C. In his reign three great events took place: (1) the Spartans waged war against their neighbours the Messenians, defeated them, and made either a partial or a complete conquest of their country, (2) the general assembly of Spartan people was explicitly declared subordinate to the council of elders, and (3) the office of the Ephors or Overseers was created.

(1) Somewhere about 650 B.C. the poet Tyrtæus was living at Sparta and wrote the lines:

$$\text{`}H\mu\epsilon\tau\dot{\epsilon}\rho\psi \ \beta\alpha\sigma\iota\lambda\hat{\eta}\iota, \ \theta\epsilon o\hat{\iota}\sigma\iota \ \phi\dot{\iota}\lambda\psi \ \Theta\epsilon o\pi\dot{o}\mu\pi\psi,$$
$$\ddot{o}\nu \ \delta\iota\dot{\alpha} \ M\epsilon\sigma\sigma\dot{\eta}\nu\eta\nu \ \epsilon\ddot{\iota}\lambda o\mu\epsilon\nu \ \epsilon\dot{\nu}\rho\dot{\nu}\chi o\rho o\nu.$$

i.e. "To our king Theopompus beloved of the gods, to whom we owed our conquest of the broad plains of Messenia[2]." The subjugation of Messenia must have been a very difficult task: the country like the other natural divisions of Greece is protected by mountains and it was defended by a brave and numerous race of Dorians. Tyrtæus tells us that one of the

---

[1] Plutarch, *Lycurgus*, 6.   [2] Quoted by Pausanias (IV. 6).

wars against Messenia was carried on continuously for nineteen years[1].

(2) We are informed by Plutarch[2] that, long after the establishment of the Lycurgean constitution, the assembly of the Spartiatæ took to a practice of distorting and perverting the resolutions laid before them by omitting or inserting clauses, and therefore the reigning kings Polydorus and Theopompus added to the constitution a new rule which enacted that "if the people chose crookedly, the elders and the kings should have the final decision[3]." Thus the general assembly was rendered incapable of insisting on measures of its own initiation: though it probably retained a right of veto on all measures which the council might propose and was consulted whenever the state had to decide whether it should undertake a great and important war[4].

(3) Plato (quoted by Plutarch) says that though Lycurgus had established a constitution of mixed elements, yet the Spartans after his time finding that their oligarchy (the kings and the elders) was nevertheless too strong and was swelled and puffed up with power and pride, set up the office of the Ephors to be a bit in its mouth: and Aristotle says of Theopompus that he reduced the extent of the kingly power by the

---

[1] Tyrtæus, Fragment 4. As the conquest of Messenia is a rare if not a unique example in Greece after the purely legendary age of a permanent conquest effected in spite of the obstacles interposed by a mountain range, it is worth while to take notice of the geography. The Spartans certainly did not cross Taygetus, whose lowest pass, now known as the Langada Pass, is about five thousand feet above the sea (Neuman und Partsch, *Physikalische Geographie von Griechenland*, p. 181 note): to the north of Taygetus they could cross without any trouble from the valley of the Eurotas to the valley of the Alpheius (see the page just referred to): but before they could reach Messenia they still had to march three or four miles up a valley with mountains on either side of it and then to cross a barren sparsely wooded ridge which unites Taygetus with Mount Lycæus. The ascent of the ridge takes an ordinary traveller half an hour, so that the height of it will be about five or six hundred feet. See Bædeker's *Greece*, p. 283.

[2] Plutarch, *Lycurgus*, 6.   [3] Plutarch, *Lycurgus*, 6.

[4] For example in 432 B.C. it was the assembly that decided on war against Athens (Thucydides I. 67 and 87). The kings however, until about 500 B.C., still had the right to engage in a foreign war, if they chose, simply on their own responsibility (Herodotus VI. 56).

creation of the magistracy of the Ephors and adds "They say that his wife asked him whether he was not ashamed to transmit to his sons less kingly power than he had inherited, and he replied: 'Not in the least: for the power will be the more lasting[1].'"

But I must pause for a moment: for there is a passage in Herodotus which in giving a rapid enumeration of the Lycurgean institutions counts the Ephors among them and is therefore in conflict with the statements of Plato and Aristotle. Herodotus was writing about 430 B.C., Plato 400—347 B.C., and Aristotle about 330 B.C.: so that Herodotus is the oldest of the three writers and, if other circumstances were equal, ought to be preferred to the others. But in this case other circumstances are not equal: for Plato and Aristotle make their statements deliberately and emphatically: Herodotus does not, but throws in his list of institutions as a sort of parenthesis, while he is thinking about many other things, and paying less attention to his parenthetic remark. These facts lead me to the opinion that Plato and Aristotle give us the true version of the oldest tradition and Herodotus does not: the opinion moreover is strengthened by the fact that Aristotle appeals to a story which must have been current long before his time and was probably older than the days of Herodotus; and it is further supported by the negative evidence of the $\dot{\rho}\acute{\eta}\tau\rho\alpha$, which in defining the Lycurgean constitution says not a word about Ephors.

It is impossible to determine what was the original character of the magistracy of the Ephors: we do not know what were their functions, how they were appointed or elected, nor for what term they held office: but, from the passages which have just been referred to, it is certain that Plato and Aristotle believed that the power acquired by the Ephors diminished the power of the kings and the elders. The name Ephors or Overseers implies that they exercised some kind of supervision over the government or some part of it.

It cannot be doubted that the three important events of the reign of Theopompus were in some way connected with one

[1] The passages are from Plutarch, *Lycurgus*, 7 and Aristotle, *Politics* v. 11. 2, 3. Bekker, Oxf. 1837. Welldon's translation, p. 392.

another. In the midst of a great war for the conquest of Messenia, it might be especially inconvenient that the assembly of the Spartiatæ should initiate proposals of its own: for the men who made up the assembly were the very same who formed the whole of the Spartan army. And again in the settlement of the affairs of Messenia it was not desirable that the kings and the council should be entirely uncontrolled, as they would have been after the assembly had been deprived of the power of initiating measures, if no Ephors had been appointed.

It is stated by Plutarch that the twenty-eight elders who with the kings formed the council were elected by the general assembly of the Spartans[1]: and the method of election which he describes is so extremely primitive that it probably belongs to the original constitution or dates from the times of Theopompus. When a councillor died the best man among those over sixty years of age was to be chosen to take his place. The people came together in assembly: certain selected men were shut up in a neighbouring building whence they could see nothing: the candidates were brought one by one before the assembly, but in an order which was unknown to the men in the building, and each as he entered was greeted with shouting: the men in the building decided that the cheering had been loudest for the man who came first, or the man who came second, or some other in the order: and the man, unknown to themselves, for whom they thus pronounced, was proclaimed as the new member of the council.

The parts then of the Spartan government from the time of Theopompus onwards were the kings, the council of elders, the Ephors, and the assembly of warriors. Until about 500 B.C. the chief power belonged to the kings or to the kings and the council of elders: the kings had the active management and direction of foreign affairs[2].

About that time and soon afterwards we meet with several reigns that might account for a diminution of the kingly power. In one of the regal houses there were Cleomenes I. (519—

[1] Plutarch, *Lycurgus*, 26.

[2] Smith's *Dictionary of Antiquities*, third edition, article Ephori, where proofs are given.

491 B.C.) and Pleistarchus (480—458 B.C.): in the other Leotychidas (491—461 B.C.). Cleomenes contrived the unfair deposition of Demaratus, was half insane for some time before his death, and slew himself in a fit of madness. Pleistarchus was a little child at the death of his father Leonidas the hero of Thermopylæ: his guardian was Pausanias, who tried to betray Sparta into the power of the Persian king. Leotychidas was brought into royal power, without any sound title, by the intrigues of Cleomenes. Whatever may have been the causes of the decline of the kingly prerogative, it is certain that between 500 B.C. and 467 B.C. the Ephors rose to supreme power at Sparta: they sat in judgement on king Cleomenes I. on an accusation of bribery, they imprisoned the regent Pausanias (about 467 B.C.) on suspicion of treason, and above all, in the year 479 B.C., it was on their own sole responsibility that they despatched the great armament to resist Mardonius in Bœotia[1]. The power which they then possessed they never lost till the decline of Sparta in the third century B.C., except perhaps during the reign of an unusually able king such as Agesilaus (398—361 B.C.).

It has already been remarked that in the period from Theopompus to about 500 B.C. we do not know how the Ephors were appointed or elected: in the time of Aristotle (about 330 B.C.) they were elected from the whole body of Spartan citizens, and no doubt by the whole body of Spartan citizens[2]. They must have been thus elected as early as the time of Cleomenes I.: for if they had been appointed by the kings or the council of elders they could not have gained that independence which they then displayed.

During the period of their greatness (beginning about 480 B.C.) the Ephors were a board of five[3] magistrates elected

---

[1] For Cleomenes, see Herodotus VI. 73-82: for Pausanias, Thucydides I. 131. 3: for the sending of the great armament, Herodotus IX. chapters 10, 11, 28: and above, page 38.

[2] Aristotle, *Politics* II. 9. 19 γίγνονται ἐκ τοῦ δήμου πάντες (they are all created from the people). *Ibid.* II. 9. 23 (αἱρετὴν τὴν ἀρχὴν ἐξ ἁπάντων), (the office is filled by election from the whole body).

[3] Aristotle, *Politics* II. 10. 6.

annually. One of them gave his name to the year[1]: they received ambassadors and sometimes at least gave them an answer[2]: they could, as we have seen, send out an armament to a foreign war and fix what troops should go, and whenever it chanced that the assembly of the Spartiatæ was called together an Ephor presided over it and took the votes[3].

The kings in time of peace were dignitaries without power: at sacrificial feasts and athletic contests they took the seats of honour and after a sacrifice the skins of the victims were their perquisite: the state provided them with regular monthly allowances of food: they superintended religious matters, and settled what Spartan citizens should be the πρόξενοι or befrienders of visitors to Sparta from the various Greek states: and they had jurisdiction about marriages of heiresses, public ways, and adoption of children: but with these exceptions all control of home affairs had passed from the kings to the Ephors[4]. In time of war the kings were commanders of the Spartan armies, and the history of Agesilaus shows that in this capacity they might gain high distinction and influence: but the expeditions of the Spartans were usually accompanied by some of the Ephors[5], who could afterwards report to their colleagues any action of the commander which displeased them.

Until the beginning of the Peloponnesian war in 432 B.C., it seems that the government, whether it was controlled by the kings, the council, or the Ephors, was faithfully conducted for the interests of the whole of the little community of the Spartiatæ. We do not hear of the rulers living in luxury, nor of inequalities or discontents among the Spartiatæ, nor of emancipations of Helots. Twice only in the course of several centuries we read that the Spartans made a new law[6]: in

---

[1] Xenophon, *Hellenica* II. 3. §§ 9 and 10.
[2] The ambassadors sent by the Athenians in their extreme distress during the occupation of Athens by Mardonius were received by the Ephors and were kept waiting ten days for an answer. Herodotus IX. 7-11.
[3] For example in 432 B.C. Thucydides I. 85-87.
[4] For the powers of the kings in time of peace see Herodotus VI. 57.
[5] [Xenophon] *De Rep. Lac.* 13. § 5.
[6] Smith, *Dict. Ant.*, third edition, vol. I. p. 915.

foreign policy they were unenterprising: and they seem to have devoted themselves to the cultivation of the military virtues enjoined by their traditions, and to looking after their interests at home, which consisted largely in keeping down, degrading and humiliating the Messenians and the other Helots.

IV. While the Spartans were waging their great war against the Athenians (432—404 B.C.) and afterwards when they were enjoying the advantages which their success procured for them, many alterations were gradually introduced in their customs and government. Helots were emancipated for service as soldiers: inequalities arose among the Spartiatæ, some of them acquiring great fortunes as regulators (harmosts) in foreign cities, others sinking to poverty and losing their civic rights: and the Ephors used their time of office for the getting of wealth and enjoyment of luxury.

Helots had been employed as light-armed soldiers attending on the heavy-armed Spartiatæ as early as the battle of Platæa in 479 B.C.: in the first years of the Peloponnesian war some of them had distinguished themselves in the field, and in the eighth year of the war (in the beginning of 424 B.C.) the Spartans, fearing they might be dangerous, thought of sending them on foreign service. This plan of removing them was not carried into effect: but a proclamation was put out that those Helots who were conscious of having done good service in the war might apply for their freedom: two thousand were selected and were emancipated with striking solemnities: but within a short time most of them disappeared, no one knew how, by secret assassination[1]. This first liberation of Helots ended in treachery and murder: but afterwards emancipations were frequently made in good faith. The men who were raised from serfdom did not become Periœci but were known as νεοδαμώδεις, or "men resembling new commoners."

Bodies of Neodamodês are mentioned by Thucydides as existing in the years 421, 418, 413, 412 B.C.[2]: and in one of the occasions where he speaks of Neodamodês and Helots as serving together he explains the difference between the

[1] Thucydides IV. 80.
[2] Thucydides V. 34, V. 67, VII. 19, VII. 58, VIII. 5.

two by remarking that "the word Neodamodês signifies that freedom has been already acquired," thus proving for certain that a Neodamodês was an emancipated Helot[1]. After the end of the war the Neodamodês became more numerous: in the year 399 B.C. the Spartans sent out a thousand under Thimbron to Asia Minor at the request of the Asiatic Greek cities[2].

In 398 or 397 B.C., before Agesilaus had reigned a whole year, a conspiracy against the Spartan government was set on foot by a man named Cinadon. Xenophon in his account of its detection says that Cinadon was a young man and vigorous in body and mind but was not one of the Equals (οὐ μέντοι τῶν ὁμοίων). When the informer was questioned by the Ephors, he said Cinadon had expressed confidence that many of the Helots, the Neodamodês, the Inferiors (οἱ ὑπομείονες), and the Periœci were in sympathy with his aims: for whenever men of these classes talked about the Spartiatæ, they could not conceal that they would like to eat them raw[3]. The story shows that the Equals were the highest of all the classes at Sparta, and that the Inferiors, being distinct from the Helots, the Neodamodês and the Periœci, were men who had been Spartiatæ but had lost their position. The difference between the Equals and the Inferiors is but imperfectly known. Aristotle tells us that any Spartan who was unable to pay his share of the cost of the public mess-table was deprived of his rights as a citizen, and many had thus been disfranchised[4]. From this we may infer that anyone who sank into the ranks of the Inferiors lost not only his vote in the assembly, which was of little value, as the assemblies were not influential, but also his right of being trained as a Spartan: hence he would have but a poor chance of rising to military distinction or of obtaining any position of importance.

When the Peloponnesian war ended in 404 B.C., the cities of Asia and the Ægean sea came under the power of Sparta. To each city a harmost or regulator was sent to establish an

---

[1] Thucydides VII. 58 δύναται δὲ τὸ Νεοδαμῶδες ἐλεύθερον ἤδη εἶναι.
[2] Xenophon, *Hellenica* III. 1. 4.
[3] Xenophon, *Hellenica* III. 3. 5 and 6.
[4] Aristotle, *Politics* II. 9. 31 and 32. Welldon, *Translation*, p. 83.

oligarchical government consisting usually of a decarchy or board of ten citizens distinguished for servility towards the Spartans and readiness to punish any sign of patriotic spirit with death or banishment and confiscation. Besides the harmosts, military detachments were sent to enforce the wishes of the Spartans in their new possessions: both the harmosts and the military commanders were harsh governors, and some of them amassed large fortunes by extortion[1]. They took home the wealth that they had acquired and thus introduced the inequalities among the Spartiatæ which were so conspicuous and so invidious in the time of Cinadon.

The supremacy which the Spartans acquired in 404 B.C. was lost again in 371 B.C. In that year an army with which they invaded Bœotia was severely defeated by the Thebans under Epaminondas; the victorious general marched into the Peloponnesus, deprived the Spartans of Messenia, and, summoning from all parts the descendants of Messenians who had gone into exile, established them as an independent people in the new city of Messenê on the site of the old stronghold of Ithomê. At the same time he founded the Arcadian city of Megalê Polis (in Latin Megalopolis) to bar the way between the Spartans and their old allies the Eleians: and in the year 369 B.C. he ensured the permanence of his work by winning the decisive battle of Mantineia. The Spartans were reduced lower than they had been for two centuries: but adversity did not restore them to what they had been before the days of their prosperity. The number of men possessed of wealth, small already, steadily became smaller, so that in the reign of Agis IV. (about 243 B.C.) the whole number of the Spartiatæ did not exceed seven hundred; of these only about a hundred were land-owners, and the rest were reduced to poverty and distress[2].

The office of the Ephors shared in the general deterioration of the Spartan commonwealth, and Aristotle (writing about 330 B.C.) speaks of it with some severity. We can indeed see from his remarks that access to the office was not obtained by bribery, for very poor citizens were frequently chosen: the

---

[1] For the harmosts see Xenophon, *Hellenica* III. 5. § 13.
[2] Plutarch, *Agis* 5.

election was conducted under a system which seemed to him very puerile, but which did not close the door to poverty. On the other hand the Ephors when in office frequently accepted bribes: and he says that on one occasion they did all that in them lay towards the ruin of the state. They often spent the wealth that they got by such dishonest means in leading a life of extreme self-indulgence, in strong contrast with the hardships which the poorer citizens endured[1].

We may now sum up the results of our observations of the Spartans and their institutions. From the earliest times they devoted themselves to acquiring and cultivating those qualities which would enable them to excel as a people of conquerors and of slave-owners: but in doing this they lost most of the other virtues, and especially the qualities which make intelligent citizens. There were few political questions in which the Spartans took any interest: they did not make new laws; they had no commerce, no gold or silver except in the treasury of the state: the only subjects debated in their assemblies were questions of war, peace, alliances, disputed successions to the throne, and the like: so that the assembly did not meet save when such questions arose, or when one of the annual elections of Ephors came round. They did not even care what men were set over them as rulers: their method of electing Ephors was childish, and the elections are generally if not always passed over in silence by the historians. Nor is their indifference surprising: for their real ruler was, not the Ephors nor any living men, but their rigid system of custom and discipline: and under that system it mattered little which of them was in command and which had to obey, since nearly every Spartan was competent to issue such orders as custom and usage dictated, and every other Spartan was prepared to obey them.

If this estimate is a just one, it follows that the really important part of the Spartan institutions was not the political part but the disciplinary: that their discipline destroyed their capacity for political activity: that the Spartans from the age

---

[1] Aristotle, *Politics* II. 9. 19-24. Welldon, pp. 80, 81.

of Theopompus till the Peloponnesian war were rather a military order than a political body: and that they and their institutions cannot be very interesting or instructive to students of Politics, except as showing how a community, which was originally political, may lose the characteristics by which political communities are distinguished.

After the Peloponnesian war the Spartans got access to rich spoil at a distance from their own country and began to think less of their common interests as slave-owners at home, than of their individual hopes of plundering the inhabitants of the cities of Asia Minor. In consequence many of the Helots were emancipated to serve as soldiers in foreign war, and the intensity of the oppression of the rest was probably diminished: while on the other hand each individual Spartan acted no longer for the common good of the Spartiatæ but for the sole good of himself, and the government was conducted in the interest not of the whole ruling caste but of that smaller number among them who had been successful in enriching themselves.

Note. I do not venture to follow Fynes Clinton (*Fasti Hellenici* vol. I. Appendix, chapter 6, page 337) in giving precise dates for the important reign of Theopompus and Polydorus and for the Messenian wars, because the passages which he quotes are taken from authors who lived after Myron of Prienê and who may have relied on his romances. There are however two genealogies of Spartan kings (Herodotus VII. 204 and VIII. 131) which compel us, unless we assume either that in one royal house the generations were extravagantly long or that in the other they were abnormally short, to place the beginning of the joint reign of the two kings not earlier than 730 B.C., and its end not later than 650 B.C. We shall probably be right in placing the first Messenian war somewhere before 700 B.C. and in the reign of Theopompus and Polydorus: the second war may be placed somewhere between 680 B.C. and 650 B.C.: but further precision seems to be unattainable.

CHAPTER V.

THE GREEK CITIES.

I HAVE already stated that between 650 B.C. and 338 B.C. the Greek communities with the exception of Sparta are to be classed as city states, or communities in which a walled city is of supreme importance and the rural districts count for very little. It seems right to place the beginning of the city states so early as 650 B.C., because at that time three out of the four communities of which we have records were ruled oppressively by bodies of magnates who lived in the cities or close to them, and who owed their power to the protection of the city walls and to the facilities for concerted action which they gained from living close to a common centre. It must however be admitted that the evidence of the great importance of the cities is not so clear at the early date which I have named as it is a century later, in the age of the tyrants.

The examination of the political institutions of the Greek cities will be divided into four parts: I. The early aristocracies and oligarchies; II. The tyrannies; III. The democracies and the later oligarchies; IV. The conquest of Greece by Macedonia.

I. *The early aristocracies and oligarchies.*

Before the year 650 B.C. the heroic monarchies had ceased to exist in all the more important Greek peoples and other governments had taken their place. Of the process of the change from the old tribal system to other systems we have no contemporary records in any case: and traditions even of a later date are absent except in regard to Corinth, Megara, Athens and Argos.

At Corinth it is said that in 745 B.C. the members of the royal family, two hundred in number, deposed the king Aristomenes, and took the control of the state into their own possession, electing one of their own number every year to act as president and discharge the functions of king. They were distinguished by their descent from king Bacchis, were known as the Bacchiadæ, and in order to keep themselves a distinct caste they forbade all members of their family to marry any one but a descendant of Bacchis. In 655 B.C., after they had ruled for ninety years, their government was selfish and oppressive[1].

At Megara we know only that the government was in the hands of certain rich families, and that eventually their oppressive rule provoked the common folk under the leadership of a man named Theagenes to rise against them and overthrow them[2].

At Athens the nobles gradually deprived the king of his power and prerogatives: and from a date somewhere between 700 B.C. and 650 B.C. the government was controlled by a permanent council of nobles, and its details were managed by nine archons or administrators, who were selected yearly by the council[3]. The council consisted of those who were serving or had served the office of archons[4], so that the council in selecting new archons also filled up vacancies in its own numbers: among the nine magistrates the first in rank was The Archon, who gave his name to his year of office: the second was the Archon Basileus, who performed the religious rites: the third was the Polemarch, who commanded in war: the other six were called Thesmothetæ, and probably attended to judicial business[5]. The nobles then from 650 B.C. or earlier were in exclusive possession

---

[1] Herodotus v. 92. Diodorus Siculus vii. fragment 9. Diodorus wrote about 20-10 B.C.

[2] Aristotle, *Politics* v. 5. 9, Bekker. Welldon, *Translation*, p. 357.

[3] Aristotle, *Constitution of Athens*, ch. 8.

[4] Plutarch, *Solon*, ch. 19, Aristotle, *Constitution of Athens*, ch. 3.

[5] Aristotle, *Constitution of Athens*, ch. 3, calls them recorders of laws or customs for judgement. The chapter may be spurious, but the assertion is probable.

of power: how they used it when first they got it, is not recorded: by 600 B.C. they were employing it selfishly for the interests of their class.

The first truly historical Athenian is Draco, who, about 620 B.C., collected the customary law of Athens and formed it, together with some provisions of his own, into a written code of legal regulations. The newly recovered Aristotelian treatise on the constitution of Athens contains a passage which also attributes to him some very important changes in the structure of the government[1]: but, as this passage was certainly either not known or not accepted as genuine by Plutarch in the first century A.D. and Pollux in the second century, though they were well acquainted with Aristotle's treatise, it seems impossible to regard it as an original part of the work[2].

Whether Draco did or did not attempt to reform the government, he did not put an end to the oppressive practices of the nobles and the wealthy. They took advantage of the harsh laws relating to debt, to deprive the poorer freemen of their lands or to reduce them to slavery: but the poor showed so much inclination for fighting that their oppressors were alarmed. In the year 594 B.C. it was agreed by both the contending classes that Solon should be elected archon and entrusted with power to deal with the existing discontents and to make a new form of government. He cancelled all existing debts, restored to liberty those who had been enslaved, altered the law in regard to security for debt, and then attempted to remedy the defects of the political system.

Solon devised a moderate system of popular government of the kind to which Aristotle afterwards gave the name of Polity. It was popular, since the mass of the citizens had a controlling power: but it was moderate, because no class had opportunities for governing in its own interest. His new institutions were the δικαστήρια or popular law-courts, the ἐκκλησία or assembly of citizens, the βουλή or council of four hundred, and certain regulations which made eligibility to office depend on wealth.

[1] Aristotle, *Constitution of Athens*, 4.
[2] Mr R. Macan in *Journ. of Hellenic Studies*, April 1891, p. 27 notices the silence of Plutarch.

The archons kept their titles and functions: the permanent council of ex-archons, henceforth known as the council of the Arêus Pagus (in Latin Areopagus), survived with diminished authority.

The δικαστήρια were courts in which large bodies of citizens sat as judges or jurymen: and Athenian citizens of all classes, including the Thetes or labourers for hire, were qualified to serve in them. The extent of their jurisdiction is not precisely known: but as they were empowered to hear appeals from the decisions of all magistrates, they had the final judgement in questions of the greatest importance: and as the laws were imperfect or uncertain, they could often be a law to themselves. Under the oligarchy there had been no general assembly of citizens or it had been as powerless as the common folk in an ἀγορή of the Homeric age: Solon ordered all citizens to come together yearly in assembly for the election of archons. The choice however of the archons was conducted by a process that was not purely elective: each of the four ancient tribes, into which the Athenian families were divided, elected from among the richest class of citizens ten candidates for the office, and, from the forty thus chosen, nine were taken by drawing lots. As Solon ordered that the laws which he had made should continue in force for a hundred years, we may infer that he intended that the assembly should for the present do little or nothing in the way of law making: but, in case it should be inclined towards unwise innovations, he established as a check upon it his βουλή or council of four hundred. To make up this council he selected a hundred men from each of the four tribes; and, to give it a restraining power, he ordered that no proposal should be brought before the assembly till the council had approved it. His rules for eligibility to office depended on a division of the citizens into four classes according to their wealth. The richest class were the Pentacosiomedimni, whose lands yielded in the year not less than five hundred medimni (about seven hundred bushels) in aggregate produce of corn, oil and wine: next came the Hippeis, who had three hundred medimni yearly and could equip and maintain a horseman for warfare: then the Zeugitæ, who had two hundred medimni and

EARLY ARISTOCRACIES AND OLIGARCHIES. 61

kept a yoke of oxen: and lastly the Thetes, who were the poorest class and worked for hire. The richest class were alone eligible to the archonship and the treasurership: the second and third class could hold lesser offices suitable to their condition: and the Thetes alone were incapable of holding places in the administration[1].

The constitution of Solon remained in full working order for only three or four years: then there arose violent contests about the appointment of archons, which show that the immediate effect of his changes had been to transfer the chief power to the nine magistrates[2]. The turbulence of factions made it impossible to enforce some parts of his constitution: but other parts of it were probably observed, and the whole served as a foundation for Cleisthenes to build upon. It is probable that the strife of classes which spoiled the working of Solon's institutions led to the restoration of some kind of oligarchy: for if it was not so, it is hard to account for the readiness of the poor citizens to accede to the wishes of the demagogue Pisistratus.

The prevalence of oligarchical governments in the Greek cities of Sicily at an early stage of their career is noticed by Aristotle[3]: the existence of similar governments in the Greek cities generally in the same stage of their progress may fairly be inferred from the silence of historians.

It is to be noticed that none of the traditions about the governments of the nobles in the Greek cities of the seventh century B.C. tell us anything about their behaviour or character when first they rose to power. From the probabilities of the case however we may conjecture that at first they were good governments and used their power well: they supplanted the long-established heroic monarchies, and could not have succeeded in such an achievement unless they had had merits of their own. It seems then that during the first part of their

---

[1] The description of Solon's constitution is taken from Aristotle's *Constitution of Athens*, ch. 5-13: except the statement that the members of the council of four hundred were selected by Solon. This is from Plutarch, *Solon*, ch. 19.

[2] Aristotle, *Constitution of Athens*, 13.

[3] Aristotle, *Politics* v. 12. 13. Welldon, p. 405.

existence they ought to be called aristocracies rather than oligarchies: for an aristocracy is a government conducted by the few best men in a community for the best interests of the whole community, while an oligarchy is a government conducted by a few for their own selfish interests. From what has been already stated about the governments of the nobles in the later part of their careers, it will be seen that oligarchy is a name which suits them precisely.

At the beginning of the chapter it was remarked that the nobles lived in the cities or close beside them, and owed their power to the protection of the city walls and to the facilities for concerted action which they gained from living close to a common centre: and it is now necessary to give authorities for the statement. Aristotle[1] speaks of the oligarchy at Athens as οἱ πεδιακοί, or inhabitants of τὸ πεδίον, a little tract of level ground near Athens, Plutarch[2] calls them πεδιεῖς in exactly the same sense, and the Etymologicum Magnum[3] a much later authority says the Eupatridæ lived in the city of Athens itself. The oligarchy at Megara were overthrown by Theagenes: and he succeeded in overthrowing them by catching them while they were taking their horses and cattle to graze beside the river[4]:—a fact which shows that when they went out into the open country they were caught at a disadvantage, and implies that they habitually lived behind defences. As to the Bacchiadæ at Corinth there is not any statement that they lived in the city, but Herodotus in a story which will be told presently explains carefully that a certain Corinthian who was not one of the ruling caste did not live in the city but in a δῆμος or place in the open country. The evidence for my proposition that at Athens, Megara and Corinth the cities as distinct from the open country were of great importance is not, I confess, very conclusive: but I have thought it sufficient to justify me in regarding the communities which lived at those places as city states and not as tribes.

At Argos the course of events was not the same as in those

---

[1] *Politics* v. 5. 9.   [2] *Solon*, ch. 13.
[3] Etymol. Mag., under the word εὐπατρίδαι.
[4] Aristotle, *Pol.* v. 5. 9. Welldon, p. 357.

cities of which I have spoken. The Argive monarchy, as we have seen[1], was not abolished but continued to exist so late as 480 B.C.: the king however was not a great power in the state: for we do not hear of any doings of any of the kings. On the other hand, the fact that the monarchy was permitted to survive shows clearly that there was no oligarchy at Argos so violent and exclusive as the rule of the Bacchiadæ at Corinth or the Eupatridæ at Athens. Since then supreme power did not belong either to the king or to the nobles, power must have been in some way divided, so that Argos had a mixed or balanced form of government: and this fact is of some interest, since it adds something to the slight resemblance between Argos and Rome which has been already noticed, by showing that in these two cities forms of government succeeded one another in the same order. In each there was first a strong monarchy: next an excessively strong monarchy or tyranny: and afterwards a mixed or balanced form of government. At Rome the three stages are marked by Servius Tullius, by Tarquin the Proud, and by the division of power between patricians and plebeians: at Argos by the early Doric kings, by Pheidon, and by the mixed form of government which was established after the decline of his power.

II. *The Tyrannies.*

The way in which the oligarchic governments were destroyed is illustrated by the successful enterprise of Pisistratus at Athens: the character of the despotisms which succeeded them by the history of Cypselus and Periander, tyrants of Corinth from 655 B.C. to 585 B.C., and by the reigns of Pisistratus and his son.

The story of the origin of the Corinthian tyranny, as told by Herodotus[2], begins when Corinth was ruled by the oligarchy of the Bacchiadæ. It was, as we have already seen, the custom of this family to forbid their children to marry any but a Bacchiad. But one of them had a lame daughter named Labda, and, as

---

[1] Above, pages 34, 35.   [2] Herodotus v. 92 and III. 48-53.

none of the Bacchiad princes would marry her, she was given to Eetion who was below the caste. Eetion had also another wife: Labda had a child, but the other wife had none, and Eetion, being discontented, sent to consult the Delphic oracle. The priestess took no notice of what he asked but declared that Labda should bear another son who should be an important person. The Bacchiadæ heard of the oracle, held counsel what they should do, and appointed ten men of their own number to go to the village where Eetion lived and to destroy the child. The ten men came to the house, went into the court and asked for the new-born infant: Labda thinking they had come out of kindness to congratulate Eetion, brought out her child and put it in the hands of one of the visitors. They had arranged that the first of them that got hold of it should dash it on the ground: but it chanced, by luck sent from the gods, that the child smiled on the man who had received it: he took notice of this, and could not perform the murder, but passed on the child to the second man, and the second to the third, and so the child was passed round all ten and none had the heart to slay it. They gave it back to the mother and went outside the house, reproached one another for soft-heartedness, and resolved to go back and carry out their commission. But it was fated that from the seed of Eetion mischief should grow up for Corinth: Labda standing by the door heard their words, and hid the child in a κυψέλη or chest: his life was saved, he received the name of Cypselus (Κύψελος), and when he was a man overpowered the Bacchiadæ, and established himself as tyrant. He drove many of the Corinthians into exile, reduced many to penury, and put to death many more. After a reign of thirty years he was succeeded by his son. Periander, the new tyrant, at first governed gently: but after he had sent an envoy to Thrasybulus, tyrant of Miletus, to ask how he could best secure his power, and had learned from the envoy on his return that Thrasybulus had replied only by going into a plot of standing corn and lopping off the tallest ears, he began to destroy the most distinguished citizens and became a more murderous oppressor than Cypselus had been.

The character of Periander's government is exemplified in

the stories of the spoiling of the Corinthian women and the seizure of the Corcyræan boys.

Among those whom Periander killed was his wife Melissa: a treasure had been committed to her keeping by a friend, and Periander after he had killed her regretted that he had not first learned from her where it was concealed. To repair his error he sent to the necromantic oracle at Acheron to question her ghost. Melissa appeared, but refused to say where the treasure was, complaining of being cold and naked, since the clothing buried in her tomb was no good to her because it had not been burned. Periander issued a proclamation inviting all the Corinthian women to a great festival at the Heræum: and when they came in their best attire, the spearmen surrounded them and stripped them of their clothes and jewels, which Periander heaped together in a pit and burned as an offering, accompanied by his prayers, to Melissa. Her ghost was propitiated, and, appearing a second time, revealed the place where she had hid the treasure.

The father of Melissa was Procles tyrant of Epidaurus. The two sons of Periander and Melissa had no suspicion how their mother's death had occurred, till at the ages of eighteen and seventeen they visited their grandfather at Epidaurus. When the visit was at an end, and Procles was bidding them farewell, he remarked "I suppose you know, boys, who killed your mother?" The elder son gave no heed to this: the younger, Lycophron, after his return to his home at Corinth, would not speak to Periander, and was accordingly driven out of his house and went to stay with friends in the city. Periander forbade them to show him hospitality; and at last, to force his son to return home, proclaimed that any one who spoke to him must pay a fine to Apollo. Lycophron, driven from the houses of his friends, did not go home but went to sleep in the open air under the porticoes. After this had gone on three nights, Periander went himself and tried to talk his son over: but got no answer except "You have incurred the fine to Apollo by speaking to me." Periander, seeing no other way of getting Lycophron out of his sight, sent him to rule over Corcyra, which was a colony of Corinth and, contrary to the usual practice among the Greeks, remained under the government of the mother city. When Lycophron had lived long in Corcyra, Periander grew old and unequal to the task of ruling the Corinthians, and besought Lycophron to come and be tyrant at Corinth, promising that he himself would go to Corcyra. Lycophron, after much persuasion, was brought to consent, but the Corcyræans did not like the prospect of the change and to make it impossible put Lycophron to death. The vengeance of Periander was worthy of a tyrant: he seized three hundred boys of the best families in Corcyra and shipped them off for Sardis to be made slaves and eunuchs to Asiatics and barbarians: the commanders however of the ships which carried them were obliged to touch at Samos, and the boys were enabled to take sanctuary and were afterwards through the kindness of the Samians restored to their parents in Corcyra.

At Athens, in the year 560 B.C., the chief contending parties were the rich men of the plain, the men of the sea-shore, and the poor men of the hill country. Pisistratus, a young Athenian who had twice won military distinction, having formed a body of partisans and declared himself to be the leader of the men of the hill country, obtained tyrannical power over Attica by means of a trick. He drove into Athens in a chariot drawn by a pair of mules, both he and his mules bleeding from many wounds, which had been inflicted with his own hands. The people were already assembled or came together to meet him. He addressed them and said he had been driving into the country and had been attacked by his political opponents: and went on to request them that he might have some men to protect him. A resolution granting his request was proposed by Aristion and accepted by the assembly: before long he and his guard of club men seized the Acropolis and he became tyrant. Twice Pisistratus was expelled from Attica in consequence of rebellions stirred up by Megacles, the head of the noble house of the Alcmæonidæ, and twice he recovered his despotic power. After his first expulsion, he bade a certain woman named Phyê of tall stature and graceful figure to array herself in a splendid suit of complete armour and drive in a chariot into the Acropolis: he sent heralds before her to make proclamation "O Athenians, give good welcome to Pisistratus: ye see that the goddess Athenê has honoured him above all men, and is herself leading him home into her own Acropolis." The people in the city were thus persuaded that Phyê was the goddess Athenê, and were induced to give good welcome to Pisistratus: he became master of the Acropolis, and his despotic power was re-established. After his second expulsion, he spent ten years in exile: at the end of that time he had contrived to amass large sums of money, and had gained the adherence of a strong force of mercenary troops and soldiers of fortune. At the head of his army he landed in Attica and began reducing the country: the Athenians marched out to oppose him but showed no vigour in their resistance: and before long he was admitted within the city. Then for the first time his tyranny rooted itself firmly in the soil. Hitherto his government had been mild and orderly: he had never tried to meddle with the habits and home life of his subjects: and, as neither of his attempts to recover his power had been vigorously resisted, his rule must have been regarded with favour by a large part of the Athenians. Now he began to rely on force and fear alone for the maintenance of his authority. He surrounded himself with a strong body of foreign mercenaries: many of the citizens from fear of him went into exile: and those who remained in Attica, in case they fell under any suspicion, were compelled to deliver their children into his charge as hostages for their good behaviour. And yet, even in this period when his government was most oppressive, he never put a stop to the election by the citizens of the nine yearly archons according to the ancient constitution, though he took care that one of the archons should always be a member of his own family[1]. At his death in 527 B.C. he was succeeded by his son Hippias, who for some years imitated the policy of his father by tolerating the maintenance of some of the popular institutions while he kept the substance of power in his own hands. After the unsuccessful conspiracy of Harmodius and Aristogeiton in 514 B.C. his rule became harsh and repressive[2].

[1] Thucydides VI. 54.
[2] Aristotle, *Constitution of Athens*, ch. 19.

The fall of the Athenian tyranny was brought about through a foreign intervention. The wealthy family of the Alcmæonidæ had been forced at the last restoration of Pisistratus to leave Athens and go into exile. It chanced that the great temple of Apollo at Delphi had been destroyed by fire, and the Amphictyonic council, composed of delegates from the Hellenic races, making great efforts had obtained money enough to rebuild it. The Alcmæonidæ contracted with the Amphictyonic council that they would for a certain sum restore the temple: and to acquire influence with the Delphic priestess they performed the task with splendour far exceeding what was required of them. After this, whenever the oracle was consulted by the Spartan state or by any Spartan, the answer was always the same "Set Athens free." In 510 B.C. the Spartans resolved to obey the commands of the god: the king Cleomenes was sent to Athens in command of a Spartan army, Hippias was expelled, the exiles restored, and the Athenians were free to establish any constitution that they might desire[1].

It was probably impossible for a Greek city, in the period when democracy was unthought of, to overthrow an oligarchy without setting up a tyranny in its stead. Tyrannies are found in all parts of the Hellenic world in or about the sixth century B.C.: at Sicyon, Megara, Epidaurus, in the island of Samos, at Mitylenê in Lesbos, in all the cities of Asia Minor, in Italy at Rhegium, and in Sicily at Agrigentum, Zanclê, Himera, Selinus, Gela and Leontini[2]. Most of the tyrants began their ambitious careers, as Pisistratus began his, by flattering the poor and oppressed classes and professing to be champions of liberty[3]: some of them however started with being hereditary kings possessing limited prerogatives[4], others were high officers of state[4], or were members of an oligarchy[4]: but all alike were usurpers of absolute power and found it necessary eventually

[1] The stories of Pisistratus and Hippias are told by Herodotus (I. 59-64 and v. 62): see also Aristotle, *Const. Ath.* 14, and Plutarch, *Solon* 30. The temple of Delphi was burnt in 548 B.C. Pausanias x. 5. 5, Ἐρξικλείδου ἄρχοντος.
[2] Grote, Part II. ch. XLIII.
[3] Aristotle, *Politics* v. 10. 4; and v. 6. 1. Bekker. Welldon, pp. 381, 382, 358.
[4] Ibid. v. 10. 6. Bekker. Welldon, pp. 381, 382.

to maintain themselves in power by employing a body guard of foreign mercenaries[1]. Pheidon of Argos, as I have already remarked, cannot properly be counted among the τύραννοι: the same may be said of Pittacus of Mitylenê with still greater confidence: for Pittacus was in no sense a usurper, but was deliberately chosen as Æsymnetes or permanent dictator and endowed with absolute power by a vote of the people[2]. If Pittacus were counted as a tyrant, Solon would have to be counted as a tyrant also: for the powers conferred on the two men were the same, and were bestowed on them for the same purposes and by the same authority and procedure.

The establishment of tyrants, or usurpers of absolute power, was necessary to the development of most of the Greek states, because nothing else would have sufficed to destroy the oppressive power of the nobles: and many of the new rulers for a time governed well and were respected by their subjects. All however in time became selfish and cruel, and being detested by their countrymen were forced to hire foreign mercenaries to protect them. But no precaution on the part of the tyrants could avail them for long in the face of the general abhorrence with which they were regarded. Their dynasties usually lasted only for one or two generations: the most long-lived of all was that of the Orthagoridæ at Sicyon which lasted a hundred years[3].

The feelings with which the memory of the tyrants was regarded in the latter part of the fifth century B.C. when Herodotus wrote his history are shown by a speech which he puts in the mouth of a Corinthian named Sosicles. The Spartans at some time between 510 B.C. and 490 B.C. conceived a project of reinstating at Athens the tyrant Hippias whom they had helped to dethrone, and requested their allies to send ambassadors to discuss the matter. The envoys of all the states disliked the proposal: it was Sosicles who expressed the feelings of all. "Surely" he said "the heaven shall be set below the earth, and the earth raised above the heaven, and men shall

---

[1] Aristotle, *Politics* III. 14. 7. Welldon, p. 145.
[2] For Pittacus see Aristotle, *Politics* III. 14. 9. Welldon, p. 146.
[3] Aristotle, *Politics* v. 12. 1. Welldon, p. 402.

have their habitation in the sea and the fishes live on dry land, if ye, O Lacedæmonians, are preparing to destroy equal governments and to bring the cities of Greece under the rule of tyrannies, which of all things in the world are the wickedest and bloodiest. If indeed ye think it good for cities to be ruled by tyrants, ye should first set a tyrant over yourselves, and then seek to do the like for your neighbours: for if ye had experienced, as we have, what a tyrant is, ye would bring before us sounder opinions on the subject than those that ye have now declared[1]." He enforced his opinions by telling a large part of the story of Cypselus and Periander: and the effect of his words was such that the envoys at the congress declared their agreement with them and the Spartans had to abandon all thought of the restoration of the Athenian tyranny.

There can be no doubt that in the age of the tyrants the Greek communities were city states, or communities in which a walled city is of supreme importance and the rural districts are of comparatively little moment. In the case of Athens, the story of Pisistratus affords conclusive evidence: for in it we can observe three times over that, so long as his influence or authority extended only to the rural districts, he was but an aspirant to sovereignty: but, as soon as he was master of the city, he was established as tyrant. And in the other Greek communities tyrannies were upheld by body guards of foreign mercenaries: and this could hardly have taken place if there had not been in each community a single fortified city of such importance that a body guard by occupying it could dominate the whole country.

Between the tyrants of the Greek cities and the tyrants of the Italian cities of the middle ages there is a close resemblance: but the tyrants, both Greek and Italian, differ in one most important particular from all monarchs who have ruled over empires, tribes or nations. In an empire, a tribe or a nation the power of a monarch always has some visible utility: in an empire he holds the whole structure together: in a tribe or nation he repels foreign attack or leads his subjects to assail

---

[1] Herodotus v. 92.

their neighbours: and above all, if his tribe or nation is successful and annexes new territory, he is supremely useful in amalgamating the people of the new territory with his old subjects. To a tyrant all these kinds of usefulness were impossible: the community that he ruled was too small to need holding together: it was too well protected by its mountain bulwarks and city walls to fear much hurt from hostile invasion: it could not hope to conquer neighbours whose defences were as strong as its own: and it did not acquire new subjects. There was, as we have seen, one momentous service which the tyrants could and did perform for their cities, and that was to put down the oligarchies and to ensure that they did not rise again: but, when once this task was performed, there was little else that they could do, and their power became a mere political survival, or an institution which exists not because it is useful but because it has existed and has not yet been removed.

III. *The Democracies and the Later Oligarchies.*

By the year 500 B.C. the tyrannies had disappeared from Greece proper from Asia Minor and from the Ægean sea: and from about that time democracies and oligarchies—the rule of the many poor and the rule of the few rich—succeeded one another alternately in most of the cities till the battle of Chæroneia in 338 B.C. put an end to the independence of the Greeks. My examples both of democracy and of oligarchy will all be taken from the history of Athens: for the march of events at Athens has been illuminated for us by Thucydides, Aristophanes, Xenophon, Aristotle, Demosthenes and other great writers and orators, while of the other Greek cities we have no knowledge beyond what can be derived from a few fragmentary notices. At Athens the period which we are considering was most unequally divided between democracy and oligarchy: the government was oligarchic only for four months in 411 B.C. and for eight months in 404 B.C.; throughout the rest of the time, a duration of nearly two centuries, it was steadily democratic.

My sketch of democracy and oligarchy as exemplified in Athenian history will be divided into five parts: (1) Moderate popular government 508 B.C.–480 B.C. (2) The changes between 480 B.C. and 432 B.C. (3) Democracy during the Peloponnesian war 432 B.C.–404 B.C. (4) Democracy after the Peloponnesian war 404 B.C.–338 B.C. (5) Oligarchies in 411 B.C. and in 404 B.C.

1. *Moderate popular government under the Cleisthenean constitution* 508 B.C.–480 B.C.

After the expulsion of Hippias a contest for power arose between Isagoras and Cleisthenes. Isagoras was a friend of the expelled tyrant: Cleisthenes, finding that he was getting worsted, made an alliance with the poorer classes and within three years after the exile of Hippias he was victorious. Cleisthenes, like Solon, devised a new system of government: and his system, like Solon's, was popular but moderate, and formed an instance of what Aristotle called Polity. He desired to grant the rights of citizenship to certain classes which did not possess them: and to this end he deprived the four old Ionic tribes of all political significance: for, as a tribe contained three φρατρίαι or brotherhoods, and each φρατρία—at least theoretically—contained thirty kindreds, each tribe was a close corporation consisting of a fourth part of the families of the Athenian citizens and would resist the intrusion of new members[1]. He divided the people, for political purposes, into ten tribes constructed on a new principle and defined not as containing certain families but as dwelling in certain demes or villages: and he enrolled in these tribes, and thereby in the list of citizens, a large number of men who resided in Attica, but were not of pure Attic descent[2]. It may be that each of the old tribes had formed a rallying point for one of those factions which

---

[1] The composition of the four Ionic tribes is from Pollux, 8. 111 (in Dindorf's or Bekker's edition). Pollux delivered his work in the form of lectures at Athens in the reign of Marcus Aurelius who died 180 A.D.

[2] Aristotle, *Politics* III. 2. 3, πολλοὺς ἐφυλέτευσε ξένους καὶ δούλους μετοίκους. Probably the text is not quite correct, but the general meaning is clear.

had produced the dissensions between localities and classes in the time before Pisistratus: for Cleisthenes took care in his new division of the citizens that the demes which formed a tribe should not lie all in one district but some of them should be urban or suburban, some situated in the inland parts, and others along the shore[1].

The whole body of Athenian citizens, greatly enlarged by the inclusion of the new citizens, formed the ἐκκλησία or general assembly in the constitution of Cleisthenes. The importance of the meetings of the assembly in the time before Marathon (490 B.C.) is proved by a passage in Herodotus in which he attributes the military successes of the Athenians in their wars with the Bœotians and Chalcidæans between 500 B.C. and 490 B.C. to their newly acquired right of free and equal speech[2]: for the right of free speech could not have produced such effects unless it were used in a general assembly.

The other parts of the Cleisthenean constitution have to do with the organisation of the army and of the council, with a strange and novel process known as ostracism, and with local government within the demes.

The military force under Pisistratus and his son had consisted of foreign mercenaries: Cleisthenes established an army of citizens. Each tribe furnished a brigade serving under the general whom the tribe had elected: at Marathon in 490 B.C. the right wing was formed by a body of troops under the Polemarch and then from right to left the ten tribal brigades were marshalled in order each under its own general[3].

The number of the council, which Solon had fixed at four hundred, was raised by Cleisthenes to five hundred, fifty councillors being taken from each tribe[4]. In the time of the Peloponnesian war, (as will be shown further on,) the council of five hundred was a committee of citizens entrusted with the duty of controlling the proceedings of the general

---

[1] For the geographical scattering of each tribe see Aristotle, *Constitution of Athens*, ch. 21.
[2] Herodotus v. 78. ἰσηγορίη.
[3] Herodotus vi. 111, whence the words are taken. Ar. *Const. Ath.* ch. 22.
[4] Aristotle, *Constitution of Athens*, ch. 2.

assembly: it considered resolutions and projects of law before they were submitted to the assembled people: the fifty councillors of each tribe enjoyed for a tenth part of the year the dignity of πρυτάνεις or presiding officers, both in the council and in the general assembly, and the name πρυτανεία was applied both to their right of presidency and to the thirty-five or thirty-six days for which they possessed it: and, as the assembly met often and had much business to attend to, such a committee was obviously necessary. The records of the age of Cleisthenes give no details about the doings of the assembly and the council: but the activity of the assembly, as we have already seen, began in that age, and it is natural to suppose that some of the later functions and organisation of the council may be referred back to this time. The opinion is confirmed by a piece of evidence from Plutarch who states incidentally that in 490 B.C. the tribe Æantis was the presiding tribe in the assembly which resolved that the Athenians should march out to resist the invader Darius[1]. It is probable that under the Cleisthenean constitution the assembly met once in each prytany.

The process of ostracism was devised to guard the state against any future demagogue who might, like Pisistratus, aspire to make himself a tyrant, and perhaps also against the recurrence of such a contest for the chief power as had arisen between Cleisthenes and Isagoras. The public assembly could, without naming any person, order that on a fixed date a vote should be taken in which each citizen might write on a potsherd the name of any man who ought in his opinion to be banished. In case the name of any citizen was found to be written on six thousand of the potsherds, he went into exile for a term of years but did not suffer any further hurt[2].

Local divisions and local governors had existed in Attica even before the time of Cleisthenes: the divisions were called naucrariæ and their governors naucrari. We know nothing about them except that each naucraria contributed two horse-

---

[1] Plutarch, Συμποσιακὰ προβλήματα I. 10.
[2] For the process of Ostracism see Grote, octavo edition, vol. III. p. 133, cabinet edition, vol. IV. p. 83.

men to the army and a ship to the navy, and that the naucrari assessed the taxation needed for these purposes and had something to do in the expenditure of it. Cleisthenes established his demes as local divisions in lieu of the naucrariæ, in each deme he set up a demarchus or president of the deme, and the demarchi took over the functions which the naucrari had hitherto discharged[1]. Beyond what I have stated we know nothing from direct testimony about the demes in the days of Cleisthenes: but there can be no doubt that even in his time the inhabitants of every deme used to meet in assembly and the assembly regulated the affairs of the deme. There had been a time when Attica was the home not of one state but of many independent commonwealths each having its own government[2] and its own divinities: and the people in the days of Cleisthenes had not forgotten the fact, for their descendants eighty years later in the time of Pericles still cherished its memory[3]. Moreover the Athenians even so late as the time of Pericles delighted in country life for its own enjoyments[4], and even then a majority of the citizens of Athens lived not in the city but in the country[5]: and if the attractions of life in the city did not draw men to desert their demes and live in Athens in the time of Pericles it is certain that nothing that the city could offer in the time of Cleisthenes would entice them from rural to urban life. From all these considerations it is clear that the rural demes in the days of Cleisthenes were well filled with a resident population: the resident inhabitants of the rural demes were citizens of Athens, and, as citizens, took part in settling great matters of state: and it cannot be supposed that they did not take part in regulating the comparatively trivial affairs of their own localities. In the time of Demosthenes about a century and a

---

[1] See Smith, *Dictionary of Antiquities*, third edition, 1891, article Naucraria. Aristotle, *Constitution of Athens*, ch. 20 κατέστησε δὲ καὶ δημάρχους τὴν αὐτὴν ἔχοντας ἐπιμέλειαν τοῖς πρότερον ναυκράροις· καὶ γὰρ τοὺς δήμους ἀντὶ τῶν ναυκραριῶν ἐποίησεν.
[2] See p. 35.
[3] Thucydides II. 14, 16.
[4] Aristophanes, *Acharnians*, the whole play.
[5] Thucydides II. 14, διὰ τὸ εἰωθέναι τοὺς πολλοὺς ἐν τοῖς ἀγροῖς διαιτᾶσθαι.

half after Cleisthenes the assemblies of the demes were fully organised bodies and had plenty of business to employ them[1].

One more change made by Cleisthenes is worth a passing notice. He ordered the archons to be directly elected, and abolished all drawing of lots in their appointment. Twenty years later, in 487 B.C., the Athenians made the appointment more a matter of chance than it had ever been: they selected five hundred, and out of this large number the nine archons were taken by drawing lots[2].

I may now give a brief summary of the political condition of Attica in the days of Cleisthenes. In Attica at that time, as in all parts of ancient Greece at all times, the population consisted partly of free men (i.e. the citizens) and their families, and partly of slaves. In matters of government the decision of great matters rested with the assembly of all the free men: but, as most of the free men lived habitually in the country and the assembly met only about once in a month, the management of current business was left to the Archons for the year and the permanent council of the Areopagus composed of Archons and ex-Archons. The government therefore was a mixture of different elements: for dealing with ordinary matters the governors were a small number of the ablest men, while for dealing with matters of special importance the rulers were the whole body of free men. In such a government there was no likelihood that either the rich citizens could oppress the poor or the poor could oppress the rich: it was in short what Aristotle afterwards called a Polity, or the rule of all the citizens conducted for the good of the whole community. There is every reason to believe that no government with precisely the same qualities existed elsewhere in Greece: for, if there had been one, Aristotle, who admired such governments beyond all others, would have mentioned it in his Politics.

---

[1] Smith, *Dictionary of Antiquities*, third edition, article Demus.
[2] Aristotle, *Constitution of Athens*, 22.

2. *The changes between* 480 B.C. *and* 432 B.C.

The invasion of Greece by the Persians under Xerxes and the subsequent maritime supremacy of Athens produced great changes in the character of the Athenian government. When the Persians had passed over the mountains near Thermopylæ, Attica lay at their mercy, and the ten generals proclaimed that every Athenian must save himself as best he could. The council of the Areopagus however contrived to provide a sum of money as an instalment of pay for men who were willing to serve on shipboard; a hundred and eighty ships were manned, and the men who served, probably about thirty-six thousand in number, received a sum of eight drachmas apiece. The Athenian fleet, which was thus provided, formed more than half of the whole Greek force that won the marvellous battle of Salamis: and the Areopagus was allowed by the Athenians in recognition of the service it had rendered to have the chief influence in the government of Athens for twenty years[1]. But the whole body of the citizens who risked their lives in winning the great battle had contributed more effectually to the result than the council that found the money. Moreover within a few years after the defeat of Xerxes the Greek cities in the islands of the Ægean sea requested Athens to be their defender against Persian attack: from being protector of the islands Athens soon became their suzerain, receiving from them contingents of ships or payments of tribute, and possessing a maritime supremacy and abundant revenue such as no Greek city had ever enjoyed: and all these brilliant achievements were due to the exertions of the poorer citizens who served as common sailors on board the galleys[2]. Athens, Piræus and Phalerum were fortified and joined together by the building of the long walls and were formed into a single city capable of containing a very large population. The result of these events was a rapid progress towards democracy: the council of the Areopagus was deprived

---

[1] Aristotle, *Constitution of Athens*, 23. The drachma contained the same weight of silver as a modern franc.

[2] For the effects of Salamis see Aristotle, *Politics* v. 4. 8. Welldon, p. 353.

in 462 B.C. of most of its powers[1], the rules which had hitherto excluded citizens of the poorer classes from holding the archonship were repealed or disregarded[2], pay was provided for the citizens whilst serving as judges or jurymen in the law courts[3], and in various ways, twenty thousand—probably a majority—of the citizens were in the employ of the state and received from it salaries or wages sufficient to maintain them[4].

3. *Democracy during the Peloponnesian War* 432 B.C.–404 B.C.

The changes which have been mentioned, together with others which have been passed over, produced the constitution under which the Athenians lived during their contest with Sparta. In the description of it we must notice (1) the general assembly and the council of five hundred, (2) the executive officers, (3) the judicature, (4) instances illustrative of the working of the constitution.

(1) The ἐκκλησία or general assembly had supreme power in all the most important matters: it consisted of all Athenian citizens who had attained the age of manhood: its meetings were held on the Pnyx, a hillside in the open air: four ordinary

---

[1] The Areopagus was deprived of power in the archonship of Conon, i.e. 463–2 B.C. Aristotle, *Constitution of Athens*, 25.

[2] Plutarch (*Aristides*, 22) says that Aristides proposed to the assembly a resolution that the archonship should be thrown open to all Athenian citizens: and he seems to imply that the resolution was passed, and that thenceforth any Athenian citizen, whether he was a Pentacosiomedimnus, a Hippeus, a Zeugites, or a Thês, was legally qualified to hold the office. It is however certain that no such extensive change in the constitution was made in the lifetime of Aristides: for Aristides died about 468 B.C. (see Clinton, *Fasti Hellenici* under the years 469, 468, 429), and Aristotle, in his *Constitution of Athens*, chapter 26, tells us that it was not till 457 B.C. that the Zeugitæ were admitted to the archonship. If then Aristides carried any resolution that altered the law, it did not go beyond throwing open the office to the Hippeis or Horsemen. The Thêtes or Labourers were never formally declared eligible: but in Aristotle's time there was nothing to prevent a Thês from becoming an archon, provided that on announcing his candidature he did not declare that he belonged to the class of Thêtes. Aristotle, *Constitution of Athens*, chapter 7.

[3] Pericles proposed and passed the payment of dicasts, during the lifetime of Cimon, probably about 450 B.C. Aristotle, *Constitution of Athens*, 27.

[4] Aristotle, *Constitution of Athens*, 24.

meetings were held on fixed days in each prytany, and other meetings for special business could at any time be summoned by proclamation[1]. Though the assembly had supreme power to make laws and pass resolutions determining the policy of the city, it submitted to certain restraining formalities. No law could be proposed in the assembly till it had been considered and sanctioned by the council of five hundred[2]: and any resolution or any new law passed by the assembly might afterwards be indicted before a popular law-court on the ground that it violated or contradicted some existing law or was contrary to the Athenian constitution. If the law or resolution was condemned by the law-court it was *ipso facto* cancelled. Moreover, if proceedings were taken within a year after the vote of the assembly, the proposer as well as the proposition might be indicted, and if the court decided against him he was subject to a heavy fine. The Greek name for the indictment was Graphê Paranomôn which may be translated literally Indictment for Illegality[3]. The Graphê Paranomôn was, beyond all doubt, the best bulwark of the Athenian constitution: though there were occasions, as we shall see, when it did not save the constitution from being violated.

The council consisted of five hundred citizens taken by lot. It was a committee to manage the details of the business of the assembly. It met on every day in the year except the religious festivals or holidays and it drew up the list of business for the assembly, determining what business ought and what ought not

[1] The place of meeting is proved by Aristophanes, *Acharnians*, line 20, ἡ πνὺξ αὑτηί, *Knights*, line 42, Δῆμος πυκνίτης and many other passages: the number of ordinary meetings by Aristotle, *Constitution of Athens*, 43.

[2] I do not know any evidence which proves directly that this rule was in force at the time of the Peloponnesian war. But we have already seen (page 60) that the rule was made by Solon, and it was certainly in force in the time of Demosthenes (366 B.C.–322 B.C.); see Demosthenes, *contra Androtionem*, p. 594, and *contra Timocratem*, p. 715, especially the words πρῶτον μὲν...πρὸς τὴν βουλήν, εἶτα τῷ δήμῳ. Smith, *Dictionary of Antiquities*, article Boulê.

[3] The events of 411 B.C. prove clearly that the procedure by Graphê Paranomôn was then an established part of the Athenian constitution: see Thucydides VIII. 67, Aristotle, *Constitution of Athens*, 29: and further on in the present chapter, p. 93.

to be brought forward. All business intended for the assembly passed through the hands of the council; and sometimes, in cases that demanded immediate action, (as in the accusation brought against the commanders at Arginusæ which will be described further on,) it had to come to important provisional decisions. The fifty councillors belonging to a tribe were presidents during a tenth part of the year: and if, during their presidency, a special meeting of the assembly was required, it was their business to summon it[1].

(2) The chief servants of the sovereign assembly were the ten generals and the nine archons. The generals were elected and not like the rest of the officers of the state taken by lot: this might be inferred from the constant occurrence among the generals of the names of distinguished men, but it is completely proved by the fact that in the year 430 B.C. the Athenians though they were many of them angry with Pericles yet re-elected him general because his services could not be dispensed with[2]. The ten generals levied troops, managed the revenue allotted to military purposes, and named trierarchs to command the ships[3]. In the battle of Marathon and in an expedition to Samos in 440 B.C. all ten generals acted as commanders: in most cases the assembly appointed a convenient number, usually three, of the generals to conduct an enterprise abroad, while the rest remained at home to manage the ordinary business of their office.

The nine archons, taken yearly by lot from among a number of men who had declared themselves to be candidates, and had submitted the respectability of their characters to a public examination, had duties of a ceremonial character and attended to the routine of some business of state, but had no political influence[4]. There were also some other functionaries for the supervision of markets and of the supply of corn, and for the

---

[1] The details about the five hundred are from Aristotle, *Constitution of Athens*, 43. An inscription of the date 410–409 B.C. printed in Clinton, *Fasti Hellenici* (vol. II. p. 345), shows how important the prytanies then were.
[2] Thucydides II. 65.
[3] Smith, *Dictionary of Antiquities*, article Strategus.
[4] Smith, *Dictionary of Antiquities*, article Archon.

preservation of order, of whom it is not necessary to speak further.

(3) The judicial bodies alone at Athens were independent of the political assembly. Jurisdiction, except in those few cases which were still brought before the semi-religious court of the Areopagus or before the first Archon, belonged to the popular law-courts which had been first founded by Solon. A large number of citizens were taken every year to serve as jurymen: they were divided into bodies varying in number from two hundred to a thousand[1], and each of these bodies sat collectively as judges to decide such cases as might be submitted to them. They sat without any professional judge to inform them about the condition of the law or the relevance of arguments: the advocate on either side cited such laws as favoured his contentions, and could use any reasoning which he thought likely to influence the court. The citizens were not only willing but eager to render their services as dicasts, partly because they received as daily pay three obols, a sum equal to half a modern franc, and partly because they enjoyed the business of the court and the importance which it conferred on them[2].

(4) The records of some of the meetings of the assembly of citizens will serve to illustrate the nature of their business. Just before the Peloponnesian war the Corcyræans requested the Athenians to protect them with armed force: the body to whom the Corcyræan envoys made their request was the assembly of citizens; on the first day the Athenians heard the arguments of the Corcyræans and of their enemies the Corinthians: on the second day they debated what answer they should give; on the third they resolved to grant what the Corcyræans desired and thereby made the great war inevitable[3]. Again in 415 B.C. the ambassadors from Egeste in Sicily, sent to ask aid from Athens, were heard in the assembly, and it was

---

[1] Demosthenes, *Meidias* p. 585, asks: "What is it that gives power and authority to any body of jurors sitting in judgement, whether they be two hundred or a thousand or any number you will?"

[2] The eagerness of the citizens to act as dicasts is ridiculed all through the play of the *Wasps*, brought out in 422 B.C.

[3] Thucydides I. 31 and 44.

H. 6

agreed on the same day to send an expedition of sixty ships[1]. In the case of the Peace of Nicias in 423 B.C. the negotiations were carried on by the ten generals, but the Treaty became binding on Athens only when it was ratified by the assembly of the people[2].

In 428 B.C. Mitylenê in Lesbos, a city allied to Athens under compulsion, broke loose from the alliance. This revolt was the work of the oligarchy, which ruled supreme in Mitylenê. In the summer of the next year Mitylenê had difficulty in withstanding the forces of the Athenians, and the rulers of the city found it desirable to give arms to the common folk. With arms went power. The common folk preferred to be ruled by Athens rather than by those among their fellow-citizens who happened to be wealthy, and declared they would surrender to Paches the Athenian commander. The surrender was effected, and the fate of the city was to be settled by the Athenians. The Athenian citizens were very angry that a city which had been in compulsory alliance with them had revolted, and, making no distinction between the oligarchical party who had led the revolt and the democrats who had restored the city to Athens, voted that every man in Mitylenê of military age should be put to death, and all the women and children sold into slavery; and they despatched a galley bearing their orders to Paches. After the vote they went home and repented of their cruelty: next day they met again, and after hearing Cleon on the side of severity and Diodotus for mercy they rescinded the order of the day before and despatched a second galley to carry the new orders. The crew of the first galley made no haste in rowing, because they disliked the work of conveying a cruel and unjust sentence: and the second galley arrived with the new orders before the first had taken any effect[3].

Judicial work at Athens belonged to the dicasteries and not to the general assembly: but the assembly also if it wished to inflict a punishment on an offender against the state could do so by a special legislative act which might be called in Latin a privilegium, and in English an attainder or bill of pains and

---

[1] Thucydides VI. 8.   [2] Thucydides IV. 118.
[3] Thucydides III. 2 and 36–49.

penalties. Miltiades, after he had won the great victory of Marathon, was entrusted with the command of an expedition of which he did not disclose the object: he used it wrongfully and unsuccessfully against the Parians, and on his return Xanthippus proposed to the assembly that he should be put to death for having deceived the Athenians. The assembly showed mercy to him in gratitude for his services at Marathon, and let him off with a very heavy fine of fifty talents[1].

In the year 406 B.C. an Athenian fleet under the command of nine στρατηγοί or admirals won a great victory over a Spartan fleet at Arginusæ: several Athenian ships which had been disabled in the action were lost in a storm which came on afterwards, and it was suspected that the admirals had made no efforts to save them. The Athenians superseded all the admirals and summoned them to Athens. Six of the number obeyed the summons. One of them was first accused in a law-court of peculation and misconduct in his command, and the court ordered him to be kept in custody, with a view probably to any further proceedings which the general assembly might choose to take. The other five appeared before the council of five hundred, which acted as a sort of business committee to the assembly, and were committed to custody.

In a general assembly, held soon afterwards, a citizen who had himself held a subordinate command in the fleet complained of the conduct of the admirals and desired that they should be punished. They were allowed to speak briefly in their defence; and the assembly did not on that day pass any resolution except that the council of five hundred should consider what course the proceedings should take, and report their opinion at the next meeting. During the interval a festival occurred at which many citizens appeared ostentatiously in mourning for relatives who had been drowned in the neglected vessels. When the assembly met, the desire to punish the admirals had risen high: the council, bringing in its report, proposed that, as the accusation and the answers had been

[1] Herodotus VI. 133 and 136.

already heard, the assembly should proceed to an immediate vote whether or not the accused should be put to death. An objection was raised that the established practice required that a separate vote should be taken about each accused person: but it was met with a clamour that the people ought to be allowed to do what it likes. The objection based on established practice convinced some of the prytaneis or presiding councillors, but eventually all of them gave way to the clamour, except Socrates the philosopher. A formal proposal was then made by a citizen, who shared the views of Socrates, that a vote should be taken about each man separately. A division was taken on this proposal, and at first it was declared to be carried: but on a second scrutiny the proposal originally made by the council of five hundred was accepted. A vote was then taken on the proposal that the commanders should suffer death: the proposal was carried and the sentence executed on the six men who were in custody[1].

The constitution, in the time of the Peloponnesian war, was arranged, in nearly all respects, according to the principles which the Greeks regarded as distinctive of ideal or extreme democracy, and tended to ensure firstly that all citizens should be equally treated in the distribution of offices, and secondly that the general assembly should be free to do as it liked. The exceptions to the prevailing tendency are to be found in the appointment of the ten generals by election, in the right of the five hundred to exclude a proposal from discussion, and in the provision that a resolution or new law might be indicted as unconstitutional before a law court. But the five hundred were not men of greater wisdom or experience than the other Athenians, being merely so many citizens taken at random by drawing lots: it does not appear from the descriptions which Thucydides gives of debates in the assembly that the generals or the five hundred exercised any commanding influence: and the illegal resolution against the admirals who commanded at Arginusæ took effect, just as if there had been no such thing as a regulation that it might be judicially indicted.

---

[1] Xenophon, *Hellenica* I. 6 and 7. He names only eight admirals recalled. Grote makes the number nine.

But it must be observed that what was an ideal democracy in the eyes of the Greeks was not an ideal democracy according to the views of our own time. When we speak of a democracy we generally mean a system of government in which the whole adult male population have some sort of control over public affairs. At Athens, a large part, it may have been half, or three-quarters or five-sixths, of the adult male population were slaves; and slaves, having lost their personal freedom, are of course incapable of political rights. If then we wish in speaking of the Athenian constitution to use terms in their modern sense and not in their Greek sense, we must say that the rulers of Athens were not a democracy but an aristocracy: it is true that they constituted a far larger part of the population than most aristocracies, but as compared with the whole they were but few. And further we may observe that without slavery there could never have been such a government as that which ruled Athens. The Athenian citizens gave a large part of their time to public business and attendance at public festivals: and they could not have done this unless there had been plenty of slaves to perform the industrial and menial work that the community required[1].

Although Athens ought, according to the modern use of terms, to be called rather an aristocracy than a democracy, it seems to be certain that the men actually and habitually employed in the daily work of government bore numerically a larger proportion to the whole population in ancient Athens than they have done in any other state known to history. The whole population of Attica may have been a quarter of a million or it may have been nearly half-a-million: the citizens numbered about thirty thousand, and it is probable that at least ten thousand of them were habitually employed in the business of government: and these ten thousand may have been a twenty-fifth part and were not less than a fiftieth part of the whole population. In modern England those who are habitually employed in governing would include members of

[1] The observations contained in this paragraph were suggested to me firstly by Professor Mahaffy, *Problems in Greek History* § 38, and secondly by Mr W. Warde Fowler, *The City State of the Greeks and Romans*, chapter vi.

Parliament, of town councils, of county councils, and of school-boards, magistrates, judges, and the staff of all Government offices, except those persons who are mere clerks or servants: I cannot say how many they would muster, all told: but, judging from those parts of England that I know best, I should estimate them at something between a two-hundredth and a five-hundredth part of the inhabitants of the country.

4. *Democracy after the Peloponnesian War*, 404–338 B.C.

In the period which followed the Peloponnesian war the poorer citizens who predominated in the assembly passed several votes to promote the pleasure and the pecuniary interests of their class. Pay was provided for every citizen who attended a meeting of the assembly or was a spectator at a religious festival and its dramatic performances. The pay was at first fixed at a low rate: before 392 B.C. it had been raised to three obols, the same sum as was paid to a dicast for a day's attendance[1]. The pay for the law courts, the assemblies, the festivals and the council came to nearly two hundred talents yearly[2]. The whole revenue of the Athenian state in the fourth century is not known: but it can scarcely have exceeded eleven or twelve hundred talents[3]: and thus it seems that about one-sixth part of it was spent in providing citizens with religious spectacles or comfortable employment.

After the three obols had been decreed, a majority more overwhelming than ever was ensured in the assembly to the poorer class. The professional orators began to devote their

[1] The decrees granting pay for attendance at ecclesia are enumerated in Aristotle, *Constitution of Athens*, 41. In the *Ecclesiazusæ*, first acted in 392 B.C., Chremes (at lines 381—2) says he had lost his three obols by being late for the assembly. For the allowance to citizens at religious festivals see Aristotle, *Constitution of Athens*, 28.

[2] See Boeckh, *Public Economy of Athens*, book II. ch. 13—14.

Supposing half a drachma was paid to 18000 spectators at 30 festivals, to 8000 citizens at 50 assemblies and to 4000 dicasts for 300 days, and a whole drachma to 400 councillors for 300 days, we get a sum of 1,190,000 drachmæ, and, as there were 6000 drachmæ in a talent, this was equal to 198⅓ talents.

[3] See Boeckh, *Public Economy*, book III. ch. 19.

skill to the purpose of persuading the ecclesia, and thus obtained a control over Athenian policy. It was fortunate for the state that in Demosthenes it found not only an orator but a patriot and a statesman: and it says much for the good sense of the assembly that it followed his counsels, unless they interfered too much with the comfort of the individual citizens. The assembly governed on the whole with moderation, and no harsh measures against the property of the rich were ever passed in it: but it insisted that the poor citizens should have their three obols for the religious spectacles, even when the money was wanted for a most necessary war to defend Olynthus against Macedonia[1]. The very frequent assemblies of the whole body of citizens gave the poorer classes a decisive voice in all questions of policy and legislation: but they also ensured that all the citizens had some knowledge of what was being proposed, and gave them the habit of listening to arguments, and of deciding questions by voting and not by force. During the period from 404 B.C. to 338 B.C. Athens was never troubled with conspiracies or seditious violence.

The fall of Athens occurred at the end of the period of which I have been speaking, and no doubt the defects of the constitution and the unwillingness of the citizens to make any sacrifices were contributory causes. But it is not certain that, even if Athens had been as well governed and patriotic as ever, it would have been able so to unite the jealous Greek cities as to ensure their independence against the new and formidable power of Macedonia.

Our materials for forming an estimate of the nature of democracy in the Greek cities other than Athens are, as I have said, very scanty. But it seems clear that most of the democracies ruled with less moderation and self-control than the Athenian democracy, and had less stability. Revolutions from democracy to oligarchy or from oligarchy to democracy recurred at shorter intervals in many Greek cities than at Athens: and sometimes, as at Corcyra in 427 B.C., and at Argos in 371 B.C. or

---

[1] Grote, octavo edition, vol. VIII. pp. 81-98, cabinet edition, vol. XI. pp. 138-157.

370 B.C., an unsuccessful attempt at revolution was punished with wholesale massacre[1]. It is to be observed that the Greek writers, in speaking of democracy, generally seem to regard it with distrust and even dislike: and this could hardly have been the case, if all democratic governments had been as well conducted as the Athenian government. We know that at Athens the whole mass of the citizens were able at any moment to do whatever they liked, subject to no restraint except from the Graphê Paranomôn and from their own characters and inclinations: and it seems certain that in every Greek city mentioned by the Greek writers as democratically governed the citizens were still more free from restraint: for many of the best and most careful writers were great admirers of artificial restraints on democracy, and if any city had provided itself with such restraints the fact would have been recorded. It is clear that a government which allows the mass of the citizens to do whatever they choose must be beset with dangers, unless the citizens have learned habits of self-restraint and mutual forbearance from a long and gradual political education. The Athenians had learned such habits, but the other Greeks probably had not: for the Athenians alone among the Greeks had had the good fortune to live under the wise constitutions of a Solon and a Cleisthenes, which, by granting to the mass of the citizens at first a very small share and afterwards a larger share in the control of public affairs, provided them with such political training that eventually they were able with safety to expose themselves to the perils of complete self-government.

5. *Oligarchy at Athens*, 411 B.C. *and* 404 B.C.

In the year 415 B.C., the seventeenth year of the Peloponnesian war, the Athenians despatched a great naval and military expedition to the distant island of Sicily. The expedition encountered many difficulties: the Athenians sent strong reinforcements: but in the year 412 B.C. their fleet suffered a crushing defeat in the Great Harbour of Syracuse, and their

---

[1] Thucydides III. 70-84. Grote, Part II. chapter LXXVIII.

army was afterwards completely destroyed. Athens itself was without any adequate defence of ships or sailors or soldiers[1]: the Athenians did their best to supply the deficiency, but there was grave reason to fear that their unaided efforts would not avail to save them, and they greatly desired to get support by making some new alliance. It was certain that no new allies could be found among the Greeks[2], and they could look for no help unless it were from the king of Persia[3].

Alcibiades, the ablest but the most unpatriotic and unscrupulous of the Athenians of that time, was in 412 B.C. an exile from his native city under sentence of death[4]. He had in 415 B.C. been appointed one of the three commanders of the great expedition to Sicily: but, when it was on the eve of starting from Attica, he fell under suspicion of having committed a great crime by wilfully offending one of the gods who protected Athens and of designing to overthrow the Athenian constitution[5]. As however there was no proof of his guilt, legal proceedings could not be immediately instituted, and he was allowed to sail as one of the commanders of the fleet: but when he reached Sicily, he found awaiting him the Salaminia, the swift galley which carried despatches, and on board of her some officers sent by the Athenian assembly to summon him home to stand his trial[6]. These officers had been instructed not to arrest him but merely to bid him come to Athens for trial: accordingly he sailed homeward in his own ship, under escort of the Salaminia. On the way the two ships touched at a port in southern Italy, and Alcibiades went ashore and escaped from his custodians: soon afterwards, getting a passage to the Peloponnesus[7], he went to Sparta and advised the Spartans how they might best defeat the Athenian forces in Sicily[8]. The charges against him were produced before one of the popular law courts at Athens: and, as he did not appear, he was found guilty and condemned to death[9].

---

[1] Thucydides VIII. 1.
[2] Thucydides VIII. 2.
[3] Aristotle, *Constitution of Athens*, 29, and Thucydides VIII. 47.
[4] Thucydides VI. 61.
[5] Thucydides VI. 26—28.
[6] Thucydides VI. 53.
[7] Thucydides VI. 61.
[8] Thucydides VI. 89.
[9] Thucydides VI. 61.

With the Spartans Alcibiades gained great influence, partly through his intimacy with a powerful man among their Ephors, and partly by the sound advice which he gave them as to the best way to injure Athens. In the year 412 B.C., at his own earnest desire, he was sent to act on behalf of Sparta in some of the cities of Asia Minor which were in alliance with Athens, and to induce them to change sides in the war[1]. Before long however the Spartans had reason to suspect that he was betraying their interests, and sent an order to the commander of their fleet off the coast of Asia to put him to death[2]. Alcibiades was warned, and, fleeing to the court of Tissaphernes, a powerful satrap of the king of Persia in the south-western part of Asia Minor, became no less zealous and efficient in opposing the interests of the Spartans than he had been in promoting them: and, after winning in some degree the confidence of Tissaphernes, he induced him to withhold a large part of the money which he had been in the habit of furnishing for the pay of the sailors in the Lacedæmonian fleet[3]. Having thus completely destroyed his credit with the Spartans, he desired nothing so much as to obtain pardon for his offences from his own countrymen[4]: for he hoped that, if once the sentence which had been passed on him were cancelled, he might return to Athens and recover some of his former popularity and influence.

Alcibiades knew that the Athenians were in a sore strait, and were longing for an alliance with the king of Persia: and in this desire of theirs and his own friendly relations with Tissaphernes he thought he saw the means of effecting his return: for, if the Athenians could only be persuaded that he was able and willing through influence with Tissaphernes to bring about the desired alliance, they would not only let him return but would welcome him as a valuable friend in their distress[5]. He believed however that his restoration could more easily be brought about if the present quiet and orderly government of Athens were to come to an end, and the city were

---

[1] Thucydides VIII. 11, 12.
[2] Thucydides VIII. 45.
[3] Thucydides VIII. 45, 46.
[4] Thucydides VIII. 47.
[5] Thucydides VIII. 47.

thrown into the turmoil of a revolution[1]. The surest way to cause political disturbance was to try to substitute an oligarchy for the existing democracy: and this accordingly was what Alcibiades did, not that he liked oligarchy better than democracy, but because he thought that any political troubles at Athens might conduce to his restoration[2]. He sought for fit agents to bring about the desired revolution, and found them among the officers of an Athenian fleet stationed at the island of Samos near the coast of Asia Minor[3].

The part of Alcibiades in the revolution consisted only in giving it a start by raising false expectations of a Persian alliance. His agents went to Athens, and there Pisander, who took the leading part among them, addressing the assembly of the citizens, urged that the only hope of salvation for Athens lay in an alliance with Persia, and declared that that alliance would be made if they would invite Alcibiades to return, abolish their democracy, which was not to the liking of the king of Persia, and set up in its stead an oligarchy which the king could trust[4]. The assembly was grieved at the prospect of losing its democratic constitution, but under the stress of circumstances gave some kind of provisional approval of the proposed change; for the present however it took no definite step beyond appointing Pisander and ten other men as envoys to negotiate with Alcibiades and Tissaphernes. Pisander remained for a while in Athens for the purpose of visiting all the oligarchical clubs which already existed there and preparing them to be ready to strike a blow against the democratic constitution: this done, he departed on his mission[5]. It soon became evident that Alcibiades was powerless to obtain help for Athens from the king of Persia or even from Tissaphernes: a breach occurred between him and the oligarchical conspirators, and he took no further part in their proceedings[6].

During the absence of Pisander the oligarchical clubs at Athens prepared the way for the success of his designs by

[1] Thucydides VIII. 48, 3, ἐκ τοῦ παρόντος κόσμου τὴν πόλιν μεταστήσας.
[2] Thucydides VIII. 48, 3, ὁ Ἀλκιβιάδης, ὅπερ καὶ ἦν, οὐδὲν μᾶλλον ὀλιγαρχίας ἢ δημοκρατίας δεῖσθαι ἐδόκει αὐτῷ.
[3] Thucydides VIII. 47.   [4] Thucydides VIII. 53.
[5] Thucydides VIII. 54.   [6] Thucydides VIII. 56.

skilfully organising a series of assassinations. The persons selected to be murdered were the most faithful upholders of the democratic constitution: the assassins were never brought to justice: and such general terror prevailed that men did not dare to mourn for the victims lest their own turn should come next[1]. Meanwhile the chief politicians in the oligarchic party, wishing to disguise their real designs, gave out that the changes in the constitution which they would advocate were moderate in character: they would limit the number of citizens who formed the ecclesia to a number not exceeding five thousand, consisting of those who were best able to aid the state by paying taxes or by serving in the war, and would propose that henceforth wages from the treasury should be paid to none but the soldiers and sailors: but in other respects they would wish the constitution to remain unaltered[2].

Pisander, on his return to Athens about April 411 B.C.[3], was eager for the establishment of an oligarchy, with himself as one of its leading members: and, even if he had wished to pause in his measures, it was now dangerous for him to do so, because, if the citizens recovered from their terror, he would be prosecuted under a Graphê Paranomôn for the proposals which he had made and carried last year, and would undergo severe punishment. One of his adherents named Pythodorus at once proposed to the assembly that it should appoint a small committee of citizens to make a draft scheme for a new constitution: Cleitophon, who was probably an opponent of Pisander, moved that it should be an instruction to the committee that they should examine the ancient constitution of Cleisthenes to see whether any of its provisions ought to be revived. The proposal of Pythodorus was carried: whether Cleitophon's instruction was accepted or rejected we do not know[4].

---

[1] Thucydides viii. 65, 66.

[2] Thucydides viii. 65, the last sentence. My small addition to the words of this sentence seems to be justified by εὐπρεπὲς πρὸς τοὺς πλείους which occurs in the next.

[3] The oligarchical government lasted four months and ended two months after new archons took office, that is to say, two months after midsummer. Aristotle, *Constitution of Athens*, 33. Clinton, *Fasti Hellenici*, vol. ii. pp. xv. xvi.

[4] Thucydides viii. 67. Aristotle, *Constitution of Athens*, 29.

Within a short time the committee had prepared its proposals. An assembly of the citizens was summoned to meet, not as usual at the Pnyx within the city, but at the hill of Colonus, more than a mile outside the walls. At this assembly the proposals of the committee were announced; and they were to the following effect. (1) Any Athenian citizen may propose whatever he thinks fit; and no proposal shall make him liable to a Graphê Paranomôn. (2) The government (that is to say, the right of speaking and voting in the ecclesia) shall be entrusted, during the continuance of the war, to a body of citizens numbering not less than Five Thousand, and consisting of those best qualified by bodily vigour for serving in the war or by wealth for contributing to the public treasury. (3) During the continuance of the war no wages shall be paid from the treasury except to the army and navy, and the nine archons and the presidents of the assembly and council[1].

The proposals bore a specious aspect of moderation, and seemed to promise that the new constitution should be something like the old constitution of Cleisthenes. The assembly gave its assent to these proposals: but, as soon as that assent had been given, it found that further and more radical changes awaited it. A motion was made and carried that a second committee of a hundred citizens should be appointed to give more precise shape to the new constitution. The report of this second committee, an elaborate document, disclosed the real intentions of Pisander and his party. It set forth a complicated scheme of government which was to come into force at some future time: but it also did what was more important by proposing that for the present a council of Four Hundred should be elected, that the Four Hundred should appoint ten generals and a secretary to the generals, and that the eleven men thus appointed should have power to do everything except alter the laws[2]. The proposals were ratified by the assembly; the council of Four Hundred, being elected during the reign of terror which had been established, was no doubt entirely filled with the adherents of Pisander, and the ten generals and their

---

[1] Aristotle, *Constitution of Athens*, 29. Thucydides VIII. 67.
[2] Aristotle, *Constitution of Athens*, 31.

secretary no doubt included Pisander himself and his most ardent partisans. No steps were taken to call the assembly of Five Thousand into existence, and thus all political rights had been taken away from the mass of the citizens, and unrestrained power was conferred upon Pisander and his fellow-conspirators[1].

The proceedings of the oligarchy which had thus been founded are not narrated in detail by our authorities: but we are told that the new rulers governed violently, and made many changes in the administration: that they "put to death some few men who seemed convenient to be got rid of, imprisoned others, and removed others from Attica[2]," that they fell to quarrelling with one another[3], and that at last they were suspected of a design to introduce a garrison of Spartans into the Piræus, the port of Athens. As soon as this suspicion gained credence the days of the oligarchy were numbered. A battalion of Athenian hoplites, employed by Pisander to build a fortress at the mouth of the Piræus for the reception of a Lacedæmonian garrison, rose in mutiny against their officers, held a meeting in Munychia, which adjoins the Piræus, to decide on their course of action, and after due deliberation marched into Athens and piled arms at the foot of the Acropolis. Many specious offers of ineffectual reforms were made to them by envoys from the Four Hundred: but they insisted on the one thing which the oligarchy most dreaded, a free assembly of the citizens to be held within the city. The citizens met in assembly at the Pnyx, and their first resolution declared that the power of the Four Hundred was at an end[4].

After the deposition of the Four Hundred, which occurred late in August 411 B.C., the Athenians had to decide what their government should be. Two courses lay open to them: they might rescind all the enactments which they had made four months earlier, and so return at once to an unmixed democracy: or they might allow those enactments, except such as were obviously mischievous, to remain in force. The second of the two alternatives was that which they adopted. They reaffirmed

---

[1] Aristotle, *Constitution of Athens*, 31, 32.
[2] Thucydides VIII. 70. [3] Thucydides VIII. 89.
[4] Thucydides VIII. 90–97.

OLIGARCHY AT ATHENS.

in substance the regulations which had been recommended by the small committee elected under the resolution of Pythodorus, and enacted: (1) That the government should be entrusted to the body of not less than Five Thousand, which they had already ordered to be created. (2) That every citizen, who furnished the equipment of a heavy armed soldier, either for himself or for any one else, should of right be a member of this body. (3) That no citizen should receive pay for any political function, on pain of being solemnly accursed or excommunicated[1]. The constitution thus established was partly democratic and partly oligarchical: it contained a preponderant element of democracy because it gave supreme power to a numerous body, who, though they were called the Five Thousand, were in reality about nine thousand[2]: but it also contained some small oligarchical ingredients, since it excluded the poorest citizens from the ecclesia, and by withholding payment for the discharge of political functions made it likely that few citizens would be able to serve on the council of five hundred and in the popular law-courts except those who had money and leisure. Concerning the motives which induced the Athenians to adopt this mixed form of government we have no information, and can only observe that the new constitution would certainly commend itself to the body of hoplites who had delivered the Athenians from their oppressors, since it gave supreme power to the class to which they belonged; and that, from what we know of the political opinions of Socrates[3], we may be sure that it met with his hearty approval and was supported by his powerful advocacy. In regard to the merits of the new government we have an emphatic testimony from Thucydides, who says that of all the governments that ruled Athens within the space of his lifetime this was the best[4]. But the mixed form of government was not suited to the needs and the condition of the Athenians: for within a few years—certainly before 406 B.C. when they con-

---

[1] Thucydides VIII. 97. 1. The meaning of the words is admirably explained by Grote in a note to chapter LXII. of his *History of Greece*.

[2] Arnold's Thucydides, note to VIII. 97. 1.

[3] Grote, *History of Greece*, octavo edition, vol. VI. p. 152, cabinet edition, vol. VIII. p. 267.

[4] Thucydides v. 26.

demned the commanders at Arginusæ, and possibly as early as 410 B.C.—they abandoned it and reverted to their well-tried system of unmixed democracy.

Within seven years after the fall of the Four Hundred, Athens was again ruled by an oligarchy. The events which led to the establishment of this second oligarchy were in one respect like those to which the earlier oligarchy owed its origin, since they began with the destruction of an Athenian fleet: but, as they were simpler and less complicated, they can be more briefly narrated.

In the year 405 B.C. the Athenians sent nearly the whole of their naval force to oppose the Lacedæmonian fleet in the eastern waters of the Ægean sea, along the coast of Asia Minor. In number of ships the Athenian and Lacedæmonian fleets were nearly equal: in all else they were ill-matched antagonists. The Lacedæmonians were commanded by Lysander, the ablest admiral ever produced by Sparta: the condition of the Athenians was such as might be expected in the year immediately following an undiscriminating execution of the commanders of the fleet. Among the six[1] admirals Conon alone was a man of ability, discipline was lax, and the operations were worse designed and worse executed than any others in the whole course of the war. Lysander took the city of Lampsacus on the eastern shore of the narrow channel of the Hellespont which divides Europe from Asia. The Athenian commanders took station directly opposite on the western shore of the Hellespont, which at this point is only two miles wide, and there anchored their ships close to the open beach of Ægospotami. The nearest place from which they could get supplies was Sestos, two miles distant: and all the commanders except Conon and the captain of the Paralus, the despatch-boat, allowed their men to go ashore and wander far inland. Lysander watched his opportunity, found the ships for the most part deserted by their crews, and captured the whole of them (a hundred and eighty in number), except the Paralus and a little squadron of eight ships under the immediate command of Conon[2].

---

[1] Xenophon, *Hellenica* I. 7. § 1, and II. 1. § 16.
[2] Xenophon, *Hellenica* II. 1.

After the battle of Ægospotami Athens could make no effectual resistance. Lysander blockaded the city by land and sea, and in the spring of 404 B.C. the Athenians were compelled by starvation to capitulate and admit the Spartans. Lysander occupied the city, compelled the Athenians to pull down at least a great part of the long walls which defended Athens and Piræus, to readmit the members of the oligarchical party who had gone into exile, and to submit to be governed by them[1]. Arbitrary power was assumed by a Board of Thirty, who, being supported by Lysander, were able for eight months to oppress their fellow citizens with violence and rapacity such as had not been experienced in Athens even under the Four Hundred[2].

The governments both of the Four Hundred and of the Thirty were too short-lived to furnish us with materials for forming any precise estimate of Greek oligarchy in general. They never went beyond the stage of being revolutionary or half-established governments: and, being in constant terror of destruction, they were obliged to resort to cruel measures which a settled oligarchy would not need. The mere fact that Greek oligarchies were often long-lived governments suffices to show that they were not, like the rule of the Four Hundred or the Thirty, so sanguinary and oppressive as to provoke successful mutiny or rebellion: and we are entitled to believe that, as Athenian democracy was the best of Greek democracies, so Athenian oligarchy was the worst of Greek oligarchies.

IV. *The conquest of the Greek cities by Macedonia.*

The division of the Greek people into a large number of small independent cities was a system which answered well enough as long as the political horizon included no states other than Greek cities and Asiatic Empires. The Macedonians were a European people inhabiting a large territory to the north of Greece, and united under a strong military monarchy. They had formerly lived under a tribal monarchy of the heroic

---

[1] Xenophon, *Hellenica* II. 2.
[2] Xenophon, *Hellenica* II. 3.

type: in the fourth century B.C. they may be compared with the Goths under Alaric or the Salian Franks under Clovis. They were devoted to military pursuits: they had some of the spirit of individual independence which is usually found in a rude people of warriors, and they showed it even under Alexander the Great, the strongest of all their kings[1]: but their king was their commander, and in time of war, so long as he commanded ably, he enjoyed supreme power. To resist such a people as the Macedonians the Greeks would have had to do the impossible: to unlearn in a moment all the maxims of jealous precaution against rival cities by which they had regulated their conduct, to give up the practice of politics in miniature and understand at once what was needed in politics on a larger scale. As it was, the old jealousy between Athens and Sparta continued to be as active as ever, only one or two Greek states joined in resistance to the invader, and after the battle of Chæroneia in 338 B.C. Greece lay at the mercy of Philip king of Macedonia.

[1] Especially on the famous occasion when Alexander did not dare to put his general Philotas to death till he had been condemned by the assembled chieftains and warriors. Grote, part II. chapter XCIV.

CHAPTER VI.

ARISTOTLE'S CLASSIFICATION OF POLITIES.

I HAVE now described, in a roughly chronological order, the different kinds of government which successively appeared in the Greek states from their infancy to their overthrow by Macedonia. I proceed to give clearer ideas both of the principles on which those governments were constructed and of the full meaning of certain terms employed in the foregoing descriptions of them, by stating the classification of polities which Aristotle gives us in his treatise on Politics. The time at which this work was written cannot be precisely determined, but part of it was certainly composed after, and other parts probably before, the battle of Chæroneia[1].

Aristotle observed all the governments that he knew, and as the result of his observation divided polities (that is to say, forms of government, or principles on which governments were constructed or might be constructed) into two classes, the right or normal polities in which government was carried on for the good of the whole community, and the perverted or abnormal polities in which it was conducted by the governors for their own private interest. Further, since he observed that in all the polities power was lodged in the hands either of one person, or of a few, or of the citizens in general, he subdivided each of his two classes into three species according as power belonged to one person, or to few, or to many. Among the normal

[1] The latest event referred to in the treatise is the murder of king Philip in 336 B.C. Aristotle died in 322 B.C.

polities the first species was characterized by the rule of one man for the good of all, and was known as βασιλεία or kingship: in the second the few best men ruled for the good of all, and it was known as ἀριστοκρατία or the rule of the best: the third, where a large number of citizens ruled for the good of all, deserved in a special and honourable sense the name of πολιτεία (Polity, or the rule of πολῖται—a Commonwealth), which was more loosely applied to all constitutions. Among the perverted polities the first species was tyranny, or the rule of one man for his private interest; the second oligarchy, or the selfish rule of the few (who in practice were always identical with the rich); and the third democracy, the rule of the many (or rather of the poor, since the poor are always the most numerous) for the selfish interest of their class[1].

The character of the several species of polity is better understood from the observation of concrete instances than from mere definition.

(1) Kingship, the rule of one for the good of all, is best exemplified in the monarchies of the heroic age of Greece, in which the kings ruled over willing subjects, came to the throne by inheritance and not by violence, and governed within the limits imposed by custom[2]. Other instances of kingship occurred in the early history of Lacedæmonia, in Macedonia, and among the Molossians: for in all these cases the kings owed their power to the gratitude of their subjects for good services which they had rendered in founding the state or in acquiring new territory[3]. Even the Persian monarchy of Cyrus and Darius, although despotic, was an example of kingship and belonged to the normal polities: for the power of the king was controlled by custom and acquired not by violence but by inheritance, and its despotic nature was merely an accident due to the slavish character of the Asiatics[4]. Beside the heroic monarchies of the Greeks we

---

[1] The classification is set forth in the *Politics* III. 6, 7. Welldon, pp. 116–120. In III. 6. 1 Aristotle defines a polity as "an ordering or arrangement of a state in respect of its offices generally and especially of the supreme office."

[2] Aristotle, *Politics* III. 14. 2. Welldon, transl. p. 146.

[3] Aristotle, *Politics* v. 10. 8. Welldon, p. 382.

[4] Aristotle, *Politics* III. 14. 6. Welldon, p. 145.

may set the governments of such kings as Cerdic of Wessex, Ethelbert of Kent, Edwin of Northumbria, and Alfred the Great: with the conquering kings of Macedonia we may compare Alaric the Visigoth or Clovis the Frank: and for the monarchy of the Persians we may find a parallel in the Ottoman sultanate of the fifteenth century.

(2) Aristocracy is constituted on the principle that power belongs to those few best men who are best qualified to use it for the good of the community[1]. The principle that power is based upon merit belongs to the best kind of monarchy, as we have just seen, and the only difference between aristocracy and this best kingship is that aristocracy gives the power to more than one and kingship to one only.

There is no instance in Greek history of an aristocracy pure and simple. The most aristocratic governments in Greece were those of the tribes in the heroic age and the government of Sparta before 500 B.C.: but all these were instances of aristocracy combined with kingship. The elders who formed the Spartan council were selected for merit and the councils were aristocratic: but the kingly power was important as well as the power of the council, and the Spartan government is to be classed as a monarchy with a large element of aristocracy.

The principle that power and merit should go together was very sparingly applied in the other Greek states, and the usual method of appointing to offices was by drawing lots among the candidates: exceptional instances of the use of voting in elections are found at Athens in the cases of the archons for a few years after 508 B.C.[2], and of the ten generals throughout the period of the democracy.

The constitution of Rome in the third century B.C. and especially after the battle of Cannæ, when magistrates were selected for merit without regard to their patrician or plebeian order, and the senate, the supreme power in the government, was filled entirely with men who had served as magistrates or been named senators for high character and ability, is an

---

[1] Aristotle, *Politics* v. 10. 7. Bekker. Welldon, transl. p. 382. "Kingship corresponds in principle to aristocracy as it is based upon merit."

[2] See p. 76.

example of almost unmixed aristocracy. The small non-aristocratic elements in that constitution were democratic or oligarchic.

It may be remarked that it is according to Aristotle an aristocratic feature in a government if officers are appointed by election and not by lot, because if officers are elected power and merit tend to go together[1]. Hence it may be regarded as an aristocratic feature in modern states that members of Parliament are elected, provided they are elected for merit: if they are elected for their willingness to give pledges, they are no longer elected for merit, and they will use their power not for the good of all but to comply with the wishes of their constituents, and the real rulers will be the constituents.

The appointment of the Premier and the Cabinet must be made according to merit and is aristocratic. The English method of selecting officers for the army and for the civil service by competitive examination is in principle aristocratic, being adopted because merit is shown by success in examination.

(3) Of Polity, the rule of many for the good of all, there are many species. Aristotle describes some of them in general terms, but does not name a definite example of any.

The first species was a form of government adopted by some Greek peoples after the fall of the heroic monarchies. In that age distinctions of class depended on military efficiency, and military efficiency on wealth. The only effective warriors were those who fought on horseback or from a chariot (we do not know whether chariots were still used in fighting, and Aristotle's words are ambiguous): those men who possessed horses, whether they served in war themselves or placed their horses at the disposal of other warriors, helped to furnish the effective part of the army; and, because they rendered this service to the community, they became the ruling class. In the Polity thus constituted the ruling class was not a large one, though larger than the ruling class in a mere oligarchy: and this species of Polity, though it was not oligarchy, had a somewhat

---

[1] Aristotle, *Politics* II. 11. 7, II. 12. 2. Welldon, pp. 91, 94.

oligarchical character. The second species of Polity was constructed on much the same lines as the first, but in a later age, when the effective warriors included not only the horsemen but also a much larger force of heavy armed infantry or hoplites. In this case, as in the other, military efficiency was dependent on property: the panoply, or complete suit of armour and set of weapons which a hoplite required, had to be skilfully wrought, and was a possession beyond the means of the poor, though it cost far less than the breeding and keep of a horse. The ruling class included every man who furnished, either for his own use or for use by another, either a war-horse or the equipment of a hoplite: and the ruling class was so large that the Polities of the second species were known in the times when they existed, though not in Aristotle's time, as democracies[1]. There were also many other varieties of Polities. In all of them, political power was shared by a class or classes which included a large part of the free men, and therefore the classes that were neither very rich nor very poor were of great political importance. The importance of the upper and middle classes might be secured by various methods: by conceding political rights only to those who had a certain amount of property, the amount being so fixed that those who had political rights were slightly more numerous than those who had them not; by giving political rights to all free men but compelling those who had property to be regular, under pain of a fine, in attendance at the assembly; or by other like devices.

The one feature common to all Polities was that they were made by a fusion of oligarchy and democracy. They were in one way democratic because they conceded political rights to a large body of free men: but in another sense they had a trace of oligarchy in their composition, because they gave more power to a man with property than to one who was very poor[2].

From what has been said it is clear that the second species

---

[1] Aristotle, IV. 13. 10, 11. Bekker. Welldon, pages 291, 292.

[2] The account here given of Polity is derived from Aristotle's discussion of it in the *Politics*, book IV. chapters 8–13 (in Bekker's edition): Welldon, pages 274–292. Nothing has been added except a few necessary explanations.

of Polity is well exemplified in the system of government which existed in most of the German tribes in the time of Cæsar or Tacitus: a system in which the assembly of the warriors, including both horsemen and foot soldiers, determined the action of the community. The name Polity may also be applied to the government established at Athens by Solon, in which the power granted to the common people was only just so much as to prevent them from being disaffected[1]: and to the constitution of Cleisthenes, in which the assembly of the citizens was supreme, but did not hold its meetings very frequently, and showed no undue favour toward the poorer citizens. And, finally, all modern governments with popular representative institutions, though they differ from Aristotle's Polity in many important features, yet have more in common with that kind of government than with any other that Aristotle recognises.

(4) We turn to the three perverted forms of government. Democracy, the rule of the many (or rather of the poor, since the poor are always the most numerous) for the selfish interest of their own class, will be considered first, because it is the least strongly contrasted with the right polities which have been already examined. The word democracy, as has been noticed above, did not always denote an extreme democracy, for there was a time when it was applied to those moderate governments which Aristotle calls Polities: and Aristotle himself is not perfectly constant in his use of the word, since there is a passage[2] in which he makes it comprehend both moderate and extreme popular rule. The democracy however which we now have to consider is the extreme or thorough-going democracy.

From many passages in the Politics we learn what Aristotle regarded as the distinctive features and tendencies of complete democracy.

Democracy was a form of government which arose in cities with a large population and a large revenue: the whole of the citizens not only were theoretically admitted to a share in the

---

[1] Aristotle, *Politics* II. 12. 5. Welldon, p. 95.
[2] *Politics*, IV. 6. 1–4. Welldon, pages 269, 270.

work of governing, but actively and habitually exercised their powers, and those citizens who could not otherwise afford the time to attend assemblies were enabled to do so by receiving remuneration out of the state treasury. And indeed such a population had more leisure than any other for attendance at the assemblies and for serving on juries: for, as their private property was small, their time was not used up in attending to the management of it. The consequence was that under this form of government the ultimate authority in the state was not any established constitution but the mass of the poor citizens[1].

Again in another striking passage Aristotle says that there are democracies in which the ultimate authority is not the established constitution but the mass of the people and the resolutions which the people chooses to make....In these democracies the common folk becomes a monarch, a monarch composed of many men, a multitude reigning collectively....The common folk, being a monarch, determines to rule as a monarch owing no obedience to the constitution, so that, becoming a despot, it esteems most highly those men who flatter it the most: and this kind of democracy holds the same place among popular governments as tyranny among kingly governments. The same temper and character is found in this democracy as in tyranny: both of them are arbitrary rulers of the better citizens, only the one rules by resolutions, the other by decrees, and the one is influenced by demagogues, the other by personal adulators[2].

In yet other passages we are told that democratically governed cities are beyond all others anxious to ensure equality among their citizens, and that the use of ostracism for the expulsion of any man, who from wealth or personal popularity or from any other cause has unusual political influence, is a result of this anxiety[3]: and when we find that the practice

---

[1] Aristotle, *Politics*, Bekker IV. 6. 5, 6. Welldon, pages 270, 271.
[2] Aristotle, *Politics*, Bekker IV. 4. 25-28. Welldon, pp. 265-267. In translating, I have taken liberties with the words but I hope not with the sense of any sentence.
[3] Aristotle, *Politics* III. 13. 15. Welldon, pages 140, 141.

of appointing to offices by drawing lots is democratic[1], we may observe (though Aristotle does not say so) that this also is a striking exemplification of the same guiding principle. When we read that the principle of democracy is freedom[2] we must, considering the tenor of two passages which have been already quoted, understand that the freedom that is meant is not the freedom of the individual but the freedom of the assembly to do whatever it pleases.

The marks then of a pure democracy as conceived by Aristotle are these: (1) All the citizens, and more especially the poor citizens, actively and habitually control the business of government, and come together in frequent general assemblies for that purpose: (2) The assembly of citizens is free to do whatever it pleases, not being bound to conform to any law, precedent, or established constitution: (3) Every citizen has, as far as the nature of things permits, an equal share with every other citizen of political power and the enjoyment of office.

It is certain that Aristotle regarded the Athenian constitution as an example of the genuine or extreme species of democracy, since that constitution cannot be brought under any of the other species which he defines: moreover he says explicitly that it is only in the extreme form of democracy that demagogues are to be found[3], and we know from history that demagogues were plentiful and powerful at Athens. But much of what he says about extreme democracy cannot be taken as referring to Athenian democracy: at any rate it does not accurately depict the democracy under which the Athenians lived. In support of these statements, I may adduce two facts. Firstly, the Athenian assembly was not in practice free to do whatever it liked, and was not above the law and the constitution. It could indeed decide in favour of an unconstitutional measure whenever it chose, and its decision was carried into effect: but the proposer of the measure acted at his peril. In case the people after accepting his proposal continued for a whole year

---

[1] Aristotle, *Politics* II. 11. 5-8. Welldon, pages 90, 91.
[2] *Ibid.* IV. 4. 23, IV. 8. 7. Bekker. Welldon, pages 265, 275.
[3] Aristotle, *Politics* IV. 4. 24-26. Bekker. Welldon, pages 265, 266.

to think it good and useful, he was safe: but if within the year his measure became unpopular, he was certain to be condemned under a Graphê Paranomôn, and to suffer heavy penalties. And secondly, the passage, in which Aristotle denounces extreme democracy for turning the common folk into an arbitrary ruler who defies law and precedent and oppresses the wealthier citizens, can only refer to cases in which the poorer classes take pleasure in reckless changes and in robbery of the rich: at Athens the assembly, though the poor citizens predominated in it, disliked changes and was considerate towards the wealthy citizens[1].

The mischiefs which Aristotle regarded as attendant on democracies have certainly been found in some governments which have borne that name. Aristotle could not have denounced them as he does unless he had seen them exemplified in some Greek democracies: in the governments (nominally at least democratic), which ruled in Paris during the French Revolution, all and more than all the evils that he describes were to be found. Athens was practically exempt from them, and we may seek causes for its immunity. One cause, the long training that the Athenians went through under the constitution of Cleisthenes, has been already noticed: the other was that at Athens the principles on which Greek democracy was founded were actually followed out in the daily life of the community, the citizens gave their time and attention to the work of government, and the people was far more truly a self-governing people than any other that has ever existed.

From what has just been said it will be seen that I regard Athens as the sole historical example of a true democracy in the Greek sense of the term. The Florentine Republic after

---

[1] For example, till 340 B.C., the richest citizens were allowed to contribute far less than their just share towards the trierarchies, which defrayed a large part of the cost of maintaining the navy; and the change to a fairer system was effected with difficulty: Grote, Part II. chapter XC.

The strong conservative tendency, which prevailed among the Athenians under their democratic constitution, was, I believe, first noticed by Mr W. Warde Fowler. There is a striking passage on the matter in his *City-state of the Greeks and Romans* (pages 170, 171).

1324 A.D. is often compared with the Athenian democracy: but, out of the three characteristics of Greek democracy, the Florentine constitution had only the two least important: the citizens had indeed, as far as possible, equal shares in the enjoyment of office, and the assembly was free to do as it liked: but the assembly was rarely convoked, and the true governors were not the assembled citizens, but some fifty citizens selected by drawing lots every two months or every four months to fill the various magistracies and boards which ruled the city[1]. In modern Switzerland some faint traces of actual self-government by the citizens can be detected in the yearly assemblies held in four of the smaller cantons, and in the cantonal and federal Referenda, or popular votes on new laws: but they are no more than traces, and do not make the Swiss government at all like the Athenian: and, beside this, Switzerland is a federal state while Athens was a city, and for that reason the two states are so unlike that it is useless to compare them.

(5) Oligarchy, or the rule of the few rich for the advantage of their own class, admits of several degrees and varieties. There is something of oligarchy wherever the enjoyment of public office is limited to those who have a certain amount of property: there is a larger element of oligarchy if the qualifying amount is fixed extremely high, or if the body of rulers fill up vacancies in their own number, or if offices descend from father to son: and the state is completely oligarchic if, besides all this, the law does not control the rulers but the rulers control the law[2]. We may detect a minute trace of oligarchy in Solon's constitution which excluded the poorest citizens from the archonship. Perfect oligarchies are exemplified in the Bacchiadæ of Corinth whose power was hereditary and set them above the law, so that they could order Labda's child to be killed, and in the Eupatridæ or hereditary nobles of Athens, whose oppressive rule necessitated Solon's reforms.

[1] Hallam, *Middle Ages*, chapter III.: in the cabinet edition, vol. I. pages 421–423.

[2] Aristotle, *Politics*. Bekker IV. 5. 1–2 and IV. 6. 7–11. Welldon, pages 266–267, pages 271–272.

Other instances of oligarchy are found in the exclusive rule of the patricians at Rome from 510 B.C. to 367 B.C., and in the monopoly of office which was enjoyed by the wealthiest class of the Romans between 150 B.C. and the time of Julius Cæsar. The most complete example of an oligarchy is found at Venice between 1310 and the fall of the republic in 1797.

(6) Tyranny, the rule of one man for his private interest, has been exemplified in the stories of the despots of Corinth and Athens. For other instances we must go to the great storehouse of illustrations of tyranny, the mediæval history of Italy where, besides the well known despots Eccelin da Romano, the Visconti, the Medici, and Cesar Borgia, there is such a host of minor tyrants that pages might be filled with a mere enumeration of their names.

We are now in a position to make some general remarks on Aristotle's classification of polities—to see in some measure what it was, and what it was not.

Aristotle defined a polity as "an ordering or arrangement of a state in respect of its offices generally and especially of the supreme office[1]": and from this definition, as well as from his use of the word πολιτεία, it is clear that he regarded a polity as the form on which a whole government and not merely a part of a government was constructed. But nevertheless he recognised that a government consisting wholly of kingship or wholly of aristocracy was, at least among the Greeks, merely an ideal or perhaps an imaginary government, and was not within the range of practical politics[2]. And herein Greek history shows that he was right: for we never find in it a whole government composed solely of kingship or wholly of aristocracy. On the other hand we find that not only kingship and aristocracy, but also oligarchy and democracy, constantly occur as forms or principles on which a part of a government

[1] *Politics* III. 6. 1. Welldon, p. 116.

[2] In the *Politics* (IV. 2. Bekker. Welldon, pp. 253, 254) Aristotle says that "speculation about the ideally best polity is nothing else than a discussion of kingship and aristocracy": and that "kingship must be a mere name and not a reality, unless it is justified by a vast superiority of the reigning king over his subjects":—a condition that can rarely if ever be fulfilled. See also Sidgwick, *Elements of Politics*, p. 579.

was constructed: for example the ancient Spartan constitution was in one part kingly, in another aristocratic, in another democratic; Solon's constitution contained elements both of democracy and of oligarchy; and even the mature Athenian democracy contained a trace of aristocracy in the selection of the ten generals for merit and not by chance. Hence it is clear that, while kingship, aristocracy, polity, democracy, oligarchy and tyranny were polities, and each of them was a form on which a whole government either real or ideal could be erected, four of them at least, kingship, aristocracy, democracy and oligarchy, were also forms on which a part of a government could be constructed, and which entered in very various combinations into the making of actual governments.

From what has been said it will be seen that Aristotle's classification of polities was based much more on philosophic theory than on history and that, in some part at least of its extent, it is not a direct classification of actual and concrete governments.

The only actual governments which it directly and straightforwardly classifies are those which were constructed wholly on the lines of any single one of the six polities, and these were tyrannies, pure oligarchies and Polities. As to the rest of the governments which Aristotle knew, it enabled him to describe them admirably, but did not help him to assign to them brief, distinctive and convenient class-names: for instance, it enabled him to describe the Spartan government as containing elements of kingship, of aristocracy and of democracy, and the constitution of the Phœnician city of Carthage as containing elements of kingship, aristocracy, oligarchy and democracy; but it did not furnish him with any class-name for either of those governments other than the single word normal or the descriptions of them which have just been mentioned[1].

It has been necessary for me in speaking of the Greek governments to employ some class-names, and the names that I have used are tribal governments and city governments. The mere fact of using these names implied an assumption

---

[1] The descriptions of the Spartan and the Carthaginian governments are given in the *Politics* II. 9 and II. 11.

GREEK TRIBES AND GREEK CITIES. 111

that the governments of the Greek tribes and the governments of the Greek cities formed in some way two distinct classes. With the aid of the Aristotelian polities and our historical examination of Greek governments we may now make some observations which will help us to see whether the assumption was justified by facts.

Firstly, it may be noticed that all governments of Greek tribes were mixed governments containing within them in combination both the rule of the one and the rule of the few, or both the rule of the few and the rule of the many: and all governments of Greek city states were pure or unmixed governments, that is to say pure oligarchy, or pure tyranny, or pure democracy (in so far as a pure democracy is in the nature of things possible). In making this general statement about the governments of city states I do not regard Argolis from the time of Pheidon to 480 B.C., and Athens in the days of Cleisthenes as city states in the strictest sense of the term: for in Argolis the central city of Argos was by no means the sole place of importance, but was counterbalanced by the two ancient cities of Tiryns and Mycenæ, and in Attica in the time of Cleisthenes the rural districts were in some respects as important as the city of Athens.

Secondly, all the governments of the tribes were limited and constitutional, and all the governments of the city states with one possible exception, were absolute or unconstitutional. These propositions might almost be regarded as corollaries to those which preceded them, since in a mixed government the various elements impose limitations on the authority of one another, and ensure that each of them shall be subject to a constitution or general understanding about the exercise of power, while in an unmixed government the ruling person or class is likely to be subject to no restrictions: but it is more satisfactory to establish their truth from history. A moment's consideration shows that the mixed governments which prevailed in the tribes of the heroic age and at ancient Sparta, as well as those in which the military class were the ruling class, were all limited and constitutional. The unmixed governments of the cities were oligarchies, or tyrannies, or democracies. It is obvious that oligarchies and tyrannies were absolute governments, and in a democracy Aristotle tells us that the ruling class, the whole body of citizens, was above the law. The one possible exception occurs in the fully developed Athenian democracy, which was in many respects exceptional among Greek democracies. It is by no means clear that at Athens the mass of the citizens was an absolute ruler. The truth seems to be that it was an absolute ruler in so far that there were no limitations that it could not throw off at pleasure, but in practice it was very much like a constitutional ruler because it voluntarily submitted to formalities which restrained its actions.

Thirdly, in the tribes, government was conducted for the good of the whole community; in the city states, except perhaps Athens, it was conducted for the good of the rulers. After all that has been said, these propositions require no further proving.

We find then that in the tribes governments were mixed, constitutional and, in Aristotle's sense, normal; in the city states they were unmixed, and with one possible exception they were absolute and, in Aristotle's sense, abnormal or perverted.

Now that we have discovered from observation of numerous instances that the governments of the Greek tribes and the governments of the Greek cities stood in strong contrast with one another, we may try to find out the causes to which the contrast was due.

In the case of tribes it is impossible to make out completely why their governments were mixed, constitutional, and normal, because we know but little about the tribes and nothing of their history. But at any rate we may observe that the tribes were militant communities engaged in a constant struggle for existence with other similar communities, and that in such communities it is essential to the safety of each and all of their members that all the classes which contribute to the fighting strength should be kept contented and zealous in the common cause, and that therefore it is necessary that none of those classes should be oppressed and that each should have its fair share in determining their common action.

In the case of city states the reasons why the governments

were unmixed, absolute, and abnormal are best seen by contrasting a city state with a larger political community: for example, England in the middle ages. In that large political community it was impossible, owing to the size of the territory, the importance of the country districts, and the diverse characters of different districts, for any single person or class to engross all power and become the sole ruler. The size of the territory necessitated the existence of local rulers or magnates, the barons: and diversities of local character made each locality inclined in case of need to act for itself under its own baron. The result was that if any person or class attempted to become omnipotent and oppressive, some of the local districts rose in revolt under their barons and the attempt ended in failure. In a city state all the circumstances were different: the country districts had no strength or importance, the power, whether it was a person or a class, that ruled in the city, met with no resistance from outside the city, and, owing to the small size of the territory, had all its enemies within its reach, and could easily destroy them unless they chose to go into exile.

In my second chapter it was stated tentatively and without proof that there is an intimate connexion between the form of a political body and the form of the government by which it is ruled. The connexion between form of political body and form of government has now been traced in the case of the Greek tribes and cities, and it has been shown that the assumption which I made when I divided the Greek governments before the battle of Chæroneia into tribal governments and city governments was one for which history affords justification.

CHAPTER VII.

THE ACHÆAN LEAGUE[1].

THE Achæan peoples of the heroic age, when they were driven by the invading Dorians from Sparta, Messenia, Argos and Corinth, took refuge in the northern part of the Peloponnesus and there founded the Achæan people of the historical period. The district in which they settled measures only about sixty-five English miles from east to west along the coast of the Corinthian gulf, and from twelve to twenty miles from north to south. It is cut off from the rest of the Peloponnesus by a range of lofty mountains which cannot in any part be crossed without difficulty. From this mountain range many ridges run northward, dividing the country into narrow valleys[2]. The past history of the Achæans and the character of their territory made them well suited for a federal form of government; that is to say, for having a single government for some purposes and many governments for other purposes. They were impelled towards union by their common Achæan race, by common experience of conquest by the Dorians, and by the certainty that, if an independent state were formed in each little valley, none of them would be large enough to be of any importance in

---

[1] The chief modern authorities for the history of the Achæan League are Bishop Thirlwall in the eighth volume of his *History of Greece*, and Professor Freeman in his *History of Federal Government in Greece and Italy*. I have compiled this chapter, after reading what those authors say on the subject, from the books by ancient writers which they cite.

[2] Smith's *Dictionary of Geography*, article Achaia: and Smith's *Atlas of Ancient Geography*.

Greece: but at the same time some sort of separate government in each valley was natural in a country where communications were so much interrupted by mountains. It is said that they lived for a time under a single government only—the kingly government of the descendants of their hero Orestes: but at some very early period each of the valleys must have acquired some sort of independence, since, on the abolition of the kingly government, at a time too early to be known to history, the separate cantons or cities acted for themselves and voluntarily joined together in a confederation, adopting at the same time institutions of a popular character. They acquired such a reputation for just government and good faith in their dealings that after the battle of Leuctra in 371 B.C. they were singled out from all the Greek states to act as arbitrators, on some points which were disputed, between the victorious Thebans and the defeated Spartans: and Polybius believed they had acted in the same capacity at a much earlier date in the affairs of Croton and Sybaris, two states which had been founded in southern Italy by colonists from Achaia[1]. For centuries they lived on, somewhat isolated from the rest of Greece and little noticed by Greek writers, but maintaining their union and their system of government. Even in the days of Philip of Macedonia and his son Alexander the Great they were left unmolested: but, after Alexander's death, some of the ambitious princes who contended for power in Greece and Macedonia contrived to sow discord among their cities: they were consequently unable to defend themselves, and some of the cities were occupied by Macedonian garrisons, while others were put under the rule of tyrants. The gradual destruction of the league which was thus brought about must, from what Polybius says, have begun at some time after 315 B.C. when Cassander came to the throne of Macedonia, and have been completed in thirty years from that date. The earlier part of the mischief

---

[1] For the early history of Achaia see Polybius II. 37-41: Shuckburgh, translation, pages 134-137. The story about Croton and Sybaris may be incorrect (Grote, Part II. end of chapter xxxvII.): but it shows that Polybius believed the good government of the Achæans had been established long before the battle of Leuctra.

was done by Cassander and Demetrius Poliorcetes, the rest by Antigonus Gonatas son of Demetrius[1].

About the year 283 B.C. it chanced that the attention of Antigonus was called away from the affairs of Greece; and the Achæans, being thus delivered from his interference, before long began to restore their federal union. At first, about 280 B.C., the renewed league consisted of only four of the cities: then it was joined by three more, and probably before long it included all the rest:—the whole number being now reduced to ten, for four had ceased to exist, and only two new ones had grown up[2]. For about thirty years the league did not include any cities outside Achaia: but in 251 B.C. Aratus of Sicyon, when only twenty years of age, rescued his native city out of the power of its tyrant by surprising the garrison, and, in order to provide for its future safety, induced his fellow-citizens to enrol their state as a member of the confederation. In the year 245 B.C. he was elected to the office of strategus or chief magistrate of the league: and that office he held, as a general rule, thenceforward in alternate years till his death thirty-two years later. He was most active and skilful in bringing cities into the league. In his second term of office he surprised and overpowered the Macedonian garrison which held Acrocorinthus, and thus set Corinth free. The liberated Corinthians were glad to join the Achæans, and the league, gaining possession of the Corinthian citadel which commanded the Isthmus, was able thenceforth to protect not only its own cities but the whole of the Peloponnesus against any enemy that came by land[3]. After this many other cities gave in their adhesion: the most important of those that joined before 227 B.C. were Megara, Trœzen, Epidaurus, Cleonæ, Mantineia, Phlius, Megalopolis, and Argos[4].

The league, throughout the period of its reconstitution in

---

[1] Polybius II. 41.
[2] Polybius. II. 41. For the names of the cities see also Mr Shuckburgh's Introduction, pp. xlviii, xlix.
[3] Polybius II. 43.
[4] For a list of the cities in the league see Freeman, *Federal Government*, pp. 713-714.

Achaia and its extension outside (that is to say from 280 B.C. to 227 B.C.), was most successful in protecting a number of Greek states from Macedonian interference. But it was never joined by Sparta nor by several other Peloponnesian cities: and about the year 227 B.C. Cleomenes III., one of the two kings of Sparta, wishing at whatever cost to regain for the Spartans their old predominance in the Peloponnesus, found that the Achæan league was an obstacle to his designs: and, having first made an alliance with the Ætolians, who might have put impediments in his way, he became engaged in a war with the Achæans, and, in the course of it, defeated them in three important battles. Aratus and his countrymen in their distress thought it necessary to ask the aid of Antigonus Dôsôn, who was regent in Macedonia as guardian of his nephew the young king: Antigonus readily granted their request, but required them in return to allow him to place a Macedonian garrison in the Acrocorinthus. He entered the Peloponnesus, and, in 222 or 221 B.C. at Sellasia in the north-east corner of the Lacedæmonian territory, the allied armies of Macedonia and Achaia won a great victory and destroyed the power of Cleomenes[1]: but the Achæans found that, by re-admitting the Macedonian power to the Peloponnesus, they had forfeited their independence in regard to foreign policy, and must conform to the wishes of their too powerful ally. The league continued to exist "for another period of seventy-five years, retaining its internal constitution, vastly increased in territorial extent, but, in external affairs, with only a few short intervals, reduced almost to the condition of a dependent ally, first of Macedonia and then of Rome[2]." From the year 146 B.C. Achaia and Macedonia were both included in the dominions of the Roman republic.

We have now to examine the structure and constitution of the league of cities or cantons[3], which, though it eventually succumbed to Macedonia, had in happier days been distinguished for sixty years of successful assertion of its indepen-

---

[1] Polybius II. 45-53 and 64-69.
[2] Freeman, *Federal Government*, p. 498.
[3] Most of the communities in Achaia and some of those in Arcadia were

dence. We will observe first the relation of each component state to the central government, and then proceed to inquire into the nature of the central government itself.

The component states were left free to manage their own internal affairs, each holding its own assemblies, electing its own magistrates, and making its own laws on all matters except the few that were reserved to be settled by the central government[1]. It is probable that they might even choose their own constitutions: but practically a state under a tyranny or a close oligarchy or even a strong kingly power like that of Cleomenes at Sparta, was excluded from membership in the league because it could not allow its citizens to take part in the general assemblies which I shall have to describe in speaking of the central government. In course of time all the cities adopted constitutions of a popular but moderate character, and in the second century B.C., when the league included the whole Peloponnesus, Polybius says that all the states employed the same laws, weights, measures, and coinage, and were all alike in their administrative, deliberative and judicial authorities, so that the whole peninsula differed from a single city only in not having all its inhabitants enclosed within a single wall[2].

The central government consisted of two deliberative bodies, the assembly and the council, and of an executive officer, the strategus, with several subordinates: its business comprised the conduct of all foreign affairs, and the management of the armed forces.

The assembly or synod was attended by all citizens of any city in the league who chose to present themselves[3]: its

rather cantons than cities: Plutarch (*Aratus*, ch. 9) calls the Achæans μικροπολῖται, citizens of petty towns. Corinth, Argos and Megalopolis were great cities.

[1] The component states were called πόλεις, and this fact alone, in the absence of indications tending the other way, is enough to show that they managed their internal affairs. For further evidence see Freeman, *Federal Government*, p. 256.

[2] Polybius II. 37.

[3] Polybius (II. 38) emphatically calls the Achæan system a democracy with free and equal speech.

business was to settle questions of foreign policy and to elect the executive officers of the league. The regular place of meeting was Ægium, a small city on the Corinthian gulf, and it seems that the assembly always met there till 218 B.C.: afterwards it sometimes came together at other cities in the territory of the league[1]. There were ordinary meetings every spring and every autumn[2]: and special meetings could at any time be summoned by the magistrates to settle important and urgent questions of foreign policy, the duration of any special meeting being limited to three days[3]. The votes on questions of policy were taken not by heads but by states: that is to say, each state had one vote, and its vote was given Aye or No, according as the majority of those of its citizens who were present inclined to the one side or the other[4].

Of the council almost nothing is known: its meetings were held not only at the times of the federal assemblies, but at other times also: for in the year 220 B.C. king Philip had an interview with the council at Ægium about a question of foreign policy, which he would certainly have laid before the assembly if it had been possible[5]. The number of members in the council must have been at least a hundred and twenty,

[1] Polybius (v. 1) says that in 218 B.C. the assembly met *in accordance with the law* at Ægium: but king Philip afterwards persuaded the magistrates to transfer it to Sicyon. The important assembly which made the alliance with Rome in 198 B.C. was also held at Sicyon : Livy XXXII. 19.

[2] For example, in 224 B.C. Antigonus Dôsôn presented himself at an assembly at Ægium in the spring and at another at the same place in the autumn (Polybius II. 54). The meeting in the spring had to elect the officers for the coming year: and the strategus entered on his duties in May, at the rising of the Pleiades (Polybius v. 1).

[3] Livy (XXXII. 22) after recording the proceedings of two days in the special meeting of 198 B.C. says " Only one day was left in which the meeting could act : for the law ordered that on the third day its decision should be made."

[4] Livy (XXXII. 22) says that in 198 B.C. when the magistrates were just going to take a vote, most of the *states* openly showed which way they would vote (omnibus fere populis...præ se ferentibus quid decreturi essent): then the citizens of Dymê and Megalopolis and some from the Argolid left the assembly: but (XXXII. 23) the rest of the *states* of the league, when asked in turn how they voted (ceteri populi Achæorum, cum sententias perrogarentur), decided in a certain way.

[5] Polybius IV. 26 προσελθόντος τοῦ βασιλέως πρὸς τὴν βουλὴν ἐν Αἰγίῳ. The business related to a question of war against the Ætolians.

and may have been larger[1]. From the little evidence that we have we may perhaps gather that the council sat for a good part of the year, and acted as a committee of the assembly to prepare the business that had to be laid before it: and, at times when the assembly was not sitting, decided any questions that were not so important as to necessitate a special meeting of the assembly.

The executive officers were the strategus, and ten demiurgi or ministers:—together with a hypo-strategus or under-general and perhaps a secretary of state[2]. The strategus was elected each year in the spring meeting of the assembly and entered on his duties a short time after his election. His office was in its origin military, and he was by right commander in the field and controller of the armed forces: but his most important functions were to act as leader in the assembly—to expound his foreign policy and obtain authority to carry it out—and to manage negotiations with foreign powers: this last part of his work was of such moment that the symbol of his office was a seal[3]. It is shown by the case of Aratus that the Achæans were more anxious that their strategus should be a good foreign minister than that he should be a good commander-in-chief: for though Aratus was a very poor general and lost many battles, his countrymen set such a value on his skill in dealing with foreign affairs that they elected him over and over again —not indeed in successive years, for the constitution forbade it—but as often as the law allowed.

The ten demiurgi were also elected by the assembly[4].

---

[1] The evidence for this is referred to by Bishop Thirlwall (*History of Greece*, vol. VIII. p. 92). In 187 B.C. Eumenes king of Pergamum offered to give 120 talents, on condition that the money was invested and the interest used to pay the councillors (see Polybius XXIII. 7 in Dindorf's edition: XXII. 10 in Mr Shuckburgh's translation). The yearly interest of a talent would be about 720 drachmæ:—a large salary for a councillor. The councillors at Athens were paid about 300 drachmæ yearly, see above, p. 51, note 1.

[2] Polybius v. 94 ὑποστράτηγος. Strabo VIII. 7. 3 γραμματεύς: but this passage proves the existence of the office of secretary only for the very early days of the re-constituted league soon after 280 B.C.

[3] Freeman, *Federal Government*, p. 299, from Polybius IV. 7.

[4] Livy XXXII. 22 Magistratus (damiurgos vocant: decem numero creantur). The words *magistratus* and *creantur* indicate that they were elected.

They acted collectively as presiding officers in the assembly and determined what questions should be put to the vote[1]: but they also acted as a cabinet or council of ministers to the strategus; for on one occasion a despatch was addressed by Flamininus the Roman general to the strategus and the demiurgi, and the reply to it was written in the name of the same authorities[2].

The federal government of the league, which has just been described, is called by Polybius a democracy: but it was not a democracy according to the definition which Aristotle gave in stating his classification of polities; for he defined democracy as the rule of the many for the interest of the poor[3]. In the Achæan league it can hardly be said that the many were the rulers: for, though no citizen was excluded by law from the assembly, the attendance was in practice limited to those who had time and money to spend in travelling to the place of meeting, and to those few who chanced to reside there. Moreover the meetings were held so seldom and lasted for so short a time that the assembly could not control the government in regard to details, and, though of course it had the supreme power in great questions and in the last resort, it practically left nearly everything in the hands of the strategus. Finally the policy of the league was conducted in the interest not of any governing class or governing person but of the community at large.

A Polity or Commonwealth was originally defined by Aristotle as the rule of the mass of the citizens for the advantage of the whole community: and he afterwards described it as a mixture of oligarchy and democracy. Hence it is clear that, on the lines of his classification, the Achæan league was a Polity. The supreme power in it belonged in one sense to the whole of the citizens, because no citizen was legally excluded

---

[1] Livy XXXII. 22.
[2] Polybius XXIV. 5 in Bekker's and Dindorf's editions: XXIII. 5 in Mr Shuckburgh's translation.
[3] Aristotle himself, as we have seen, in one passage uses the term democracy to denote any government in which a large number of citizens take part: but in doing so he departs from his original definition of it.

from the assembly, and thus the constitution had one of the characteristics of democracy: but in another sense power belonged to those only of the citizens who possessed a fair income and could actually attend the meetings, and in this respect the constitution was oligarchic. Moreover, though oligarchy and democracy when unmixed both belong to the perverted polities, because their governments rule selfishly, the mixture of them in the Achæan league produced a normal polity, viz., a Polity or Commonwealth, whose governors ruled for the good of the whole people. But these were not the only elements in the constitution: the aristocratic principle was conspicuously present, and was seen in the great power and commanding influence which Aratus possessed in consequence of his high qualifications as a ruler and adviser.

The federal system of government combined many advantages. It enabled the Greeks to continue to live as members of small self-governing communities—a way of living to which the physical features of their country naturally led them, and to which they were deeply attached: it gave them, through their union, much greater security than they could have enjoyed without it: and it formed a large part of them into a community that more resembled a nation than anything else that had yet arisen in Greece. The system was tried not only by the Achæans but also by several other divisions of the Hellenic race: by the Phocians, the Acarnanians, the Epirots, the Arcadians, and the Ætolians[1]: and among the Ætolians and Acarnanians it attained such a measure of success that in the later period of the Macedonian supremacy these two peoples were, after the Achæans, the most important of the Hellenic powers.

[1] See Professor Freeman's *History of Federal Government*.

www.ingramcontent.com/pod-product-compliance
Lightning Source LLC
Chambersburg PA
CBHW030901170426
43193CB00009BA/704